Leasing Lessons
for Smart Shoppers

Leasing Lessons for Smart Shoppers

Mark Eskeldson

Technews Publishing

Fair Oaks, CA

Library of Congress Catalog Card Number: 97-90048

ISBN: 0-9640560-4-6

Published by
Technews Publishing, a division of Technews Corp.,
7840 Madison Avenue, Suite 185, Fair Oaks, CA 95628

FIRST EDITION

1st Printing

Manufactured in the United States of America.

Cover Design by Paula Schlosser

DEDICATION

This book is dedicated to the salespeople who were persecuted for refusing to cheat their customers. And to the honest car dealers and salespeople across the country who are tired of the "morally-challenged" ones giving their industry a bad name.

ABOUT THE AUTHOR

Mark Eskeldson is the author of *What Auto Mechanics Don't Want You to Know*, the first hard-hitting exposé of the auto repair industry. His books have been featured in *Smart Money, Reader's Digest, Kiplinger's, The Wall Street Journal,* and on ABC-TV.

ACKNOWLEDGMENTS

This book would not have been possible without the help and cooperation of many people. My special thanks to those in the auto industry who provided tips and documents on the Ford leasing story. For obvious reasons, I cannot thank them here by name, but I am deeply indebted to them and applaud their integrity. The car business needs more people like them.

Contents

Introduction

Consumer advocate and auto expert Mark Eskeldson has done it again. In September of 1991, he was on the radio exposing fraud at Sears Auto Centers—and in June of 1992 the national newswires announced that Sears had just been busted. His last book, *What Auto Mechanics Don't Want You to Know,* exposed similar practices at some of the biggest names in the auto repair industry.

Now he's blowing the lid off what could turn out to be the biggest consumer fraud of the decade: deceptive sales practices that were taught nationwide, over a period of at least six years, to dealers and salespeople representing the second largest automaker in the country.

The author has their training manuals and quotes from them in a shocking chapter on Ford's leasing practices. You'll read how salesmen were taught to trick people into leases, and how to conceal actual selling prices so overcharges would not be discovered. You'll read how former salespeople have testified to these practices, and you'll read about actual victims who were cheated because of them.

For all those who are thinking about leasing, this book reveals everything you need to know—from how to avoid overcharges to where you can find those "secret numbers" that will help you get the best possible deal.

And you'll learn about *LeaseWise,* the only national service that provides competitive bidding to help consumers get the lowest prices on new-car leases. *LeaseWise* is a new program from CarBargains, the non-profit car-buying service, and is the only program of its kind in the country. And *Leasing Lessons* is the only book of its kind that mentions it.

NOTE: The term "salesman" was used to improve readability and was not intended as a slight to the female salespeople of the auto industry.

The author is well aware of the inroads that women have made in this business: While he was "undercover" last year in Phoenix, Laura the Lease Manager showed him that the ladies can run a leasing scam as well as any man—maybe better.

1

How Leasing Works:
The Pros & Cons

Advertising for new-car leases has spread like wildfire—
it's all over TV, radio, and most newspapers. And the ads
make them sound so attractive, with low monthly payments and sometimes even "zero down." Compared to
the higher payments of a conventional purchase, it's no
wonder more and more people are leasing every year!
But is it really "cheaper," or is there more to leasing than
meets the eye?

Dealers and salespeople claim that leasing is the
"smart" way to drive a car, using lines such as, "Leasing
is simple—instead of paying for the whole car, you only
pay for the part you use."

Others aren't so sure—consumer advocates and state prosecutors have warned that many people are getting ripped off. In a 1994 story, the *Detroit Free Press* quoted Ralph Nader as saying, "Consumers are getting gouged far too often...It's more like auto fleecing than leasing." And in a September, 1996 *Wall Street Journal* article on leasing, Florida Assistant Attorney General Jack Norris said, "Consumers are getting robbed."

So who's right, the dealers or the consumer watchdogs? They both are. Many people have gotten great lease deals, and many others have been robbed. The ones in the middle ended up with deals that they probably wouldn't have agreed to, had they really understood what was involved in their transactions.

As you'll see in the next two chapters, there have been a lot of dirty tricks—and outright fraud—in the sales end of the leasing business. But I'm going to teach the secrets of leasing to as many people as possible, making it a lot harder for dishonest salespeople to cheat customers out of their hard-earned money.

So read on, as I explain how leasing works. And when you're done with this book, you'll know a lot more about leasing than most dealers (and automakers) want you to know.

Why Dealers (and Automakers) Love Leasing

New-car dealers love leasing for the same reasons that automakers love it: leasing allows them to move a lot more new cars than they would be able to with conventional financing. Since there's no ownership at the end of a lease, people have to go back to the dealer more often, so the shorter the lease term, the more chances dealers get to make money off the same customers.

Leasing also allows people to drive more expensive

vehicles than they could purchase, so dealers and auto-makers are able to move more higher-priced cars. (In fact, if it wasn't for leasing, the luxury-car market might have vanished by now.)

The dealers have another reason to love leasing, and it's a big one for those who are not particularly honest: Leasing allows dealers to make a lot more money off their customers because few of them understand it. The head of a large lease training company admitted this when he said, "There is an opportunity to take advantage of the customer in a lease because the focus is on (month-ly) payments, not price." *Remember those words.*

Why Leasing Companies Love Leasing

Leasing companies (including the ones that are owned by automakers) have two reasons to love leasing. First, it allows them to make a lot more interest on every car they finance, since less principal is being paid off in every lease payment.

For example, on $20,000 loan and lease balances, at 8% for 3 years (50% residual on the lease), total finance charges on the lease would be $3,608. On the loan, total finance charges would only be $2,572. So you would pay $1,036 more in finance charges over 3 years on the lease, compared to a 3-year loan. The interest on this 3-year lease is just a little less than the total interest that would be paid on a 5-year loan (same APR).

Paying off less principal in a lease lowers the monthly payment dramatically, but it also causes higher finance charges. This is why credit card companies encourage people to make only minimum payments—they get more finance charges that way. And that's one of the dirty little secrets of leasing: *It's the automotive version of minimum payments on a credit card.*

Leasing companies are also able to make more interest because they are not required to disclose the effective APR that's being charged. (So they don't.) Because of this loophole, a lot of leasing companies charge higher interest rates on leases than they do on loans. (They have to disclose those.) This is especially true of leasing companies owned by automakers.

As if those reasons weren't enough, there's one more: Because they are the legal owners of the leased vehicles, leasing companies get to write off all the depreciation— even though the depreciation is being paid by their customers. *No wonder they think everyone should lease.*

Leasing: What It Is (& Isn't)

No matter what a salesman tells you, leasing is essentially a long-term rental agreement that may (or may not) have a purchase option at the end. There is no ownership or equity involved, unless you exercise your purchase option and buy the vehicle. Since the purchase option price is usually around 50-60% of the original MSRP, this could be a lot of money to come up with at the end of a lease.

The factors that are used to determine monthly lease payments are: the selling price of the vehicle, the amount of the down payment, the length of the lease, the interest rate, and the estimated wholesale value of the car at the end. (Chapter 4 and the tables in the Appendix show how these factors affect lease payments.)

Most people who lease don't really understand how it works, so they fail to negotiate. The result: bigger down payments and higher monthly payments than a "smart shopper" would pay. (Be sure to read Chapter 6.) *The more you know, the better deal you will get.*

Open-end leases are really high-stakes gambling. If you agree to one of these, make sure you have a lot of money that you can afford to lose, because you'll be responsible for all "excess" depreciation at the end of the lease, no matter how much it is. (If the market value of your vehicle drops $10,000 because *Consumer Reports* does a negative story about it, that becomes your loss.) Unless you're a real gambler, make sure it's a closed-end lease before signing any contracts.

Advantages of Leasing

At least in theory, short-term leasing offers the following advantages: less total cash tied up in a vehicle, lower down payments and monthly payments, no trade-in or selling inconvenience, and protection against big losses due to depreciation. And if you can get a lease that has a large factory subsidy, you could end up with a good deal.

Disadvantages of Leasing

If you decide to sell the car or turn it in before the end of the lease, you'll have to pay a substantial penalty for early termination. This includes accidental termination, such as a stolen or totaled car, so be sure to get gap insurance to cover the amount owed that exceeds your insurance.

The early termination penalty is usually the difference between the unpaid depreciation and the auction value of the car, but in some cases, you may be required to make all the remaining payments. Depending on how early you terminate, this could be as much as $5,000 on a $20,000 car. If you can't afford this, you shouldn't be leasing.

Leasing usually requires a $100,000/$300,000 liability policy, which may cost a lot more than the level of insurance you're used to carrying. You'll have to pay extra for excess mileage, poor maintenance, and physical damage (unusual wear) at the end of the lease. And your total cost of driving (long-term) will usually be higher on a lease than a conventional purchase, especially if the purchased car is kept for at least 4 years.

Finally, unless you decide to end the renewal cycle by purchasing, you will always be making car payments. If you like "paying things off," leasing is not for you.

The Best Candidates for a Lease

The best candidates for a lease are people who would normally get a new car every 2-3 years, and are not particularly concerned about the higher long-term costs of that practice. Luxury-car buyers are usually good candidates for leases because automakers frequently offer subsidized leases with reduced down payments and dramatically lower monthly payments.

If you're tempted to get one of those new electric cars, be sure to lease it. Their batteries currently cost about $15,000 and you wouldn't want to be stuck with that bill.

The Worst Candidates for a Lease

The worst candidate for a lease: someone who can't afford to pay an early termination penalty. For this reason, leasing is not a prudent choice for someone who's financially strapped. (They should buy a good used car.)

The second worst candidate: someone who wants to end up owning the vehicle. Buying a car at the end defeats the purpose of leasing, which is to drive a new car every 2-3 years with no trade-in hassles. And if a lease deal was a good one to begin with (i.e., low monthly payments with a high residual), the car usually won't be worth buying at the residual/purchase option price.

Other poor candidates: people who drive a lot of miles (over 15,000 miles per year), and those who fail to take good care of their cars.

Leasing Terminology

Before you move on to the other chapters, be sure to read the following terms and definitions so you will be able to understand the unusual language of leasing.

Acquisition fee: Fee charged by the leasing company to buy a vehicle and set up the lease. Sometimes negotiable. Also called "initiation fee." Typical charge: $450

Cap cost or Capitalized cost: The price of the car; what the leasing company is paying the dealer for the car. This is almost always negotiable. The lower this figure is, the lower your payments will be.

Cap reduction: Any down payment, trade-in, or rebate that reduces the cap cost (total amount leased). A larger cap reduction should reduce your monthly payment and cut your financing costs.

Closed-end lease: Leasing company assumes all risk for drop in value due to excess depreciation. Customer can just walk away at end of lease. (Preferred type)

Depreciation: The difference between the net cap cost and the residual. Represents loss of market value.

Disposition fee: Fee charged at the end of a lease for turning in the vehicle. Negotiate this *before* signing the lease—only agree to pay an acquisition fee *or* a disposition fee, not both. Typical charge: $200-400

Early termination penalty: The price you'll pay to end your lease early. Ask what this is in advance: it's usually thousands of dollars.

Excess mileage charge: Additional charge at the end of a lease for exceeding the mileage limit. Usually 15 cents per mile. Watch out for low-mileage leases—this charge could end up costing over a thousand dollars.

Gap insurance: Policy to cover the difference between the balance owed on a lease and normal insurance coverage. Needed in case of theft or total loss due to accident. This should be included in the lease—insist on it.

Initiation fee: Same as "acquisition fee."

Lease rate: Monthly rate charged by leasing company, similar to interest rate. Includes both interest and profit. Lease rate = [net cap cost + residual] x money factor

Lessee: The one who is leasing a vehicle (the customer).

Lessor: The lender/leasing company.

Mileage allowance: The number of miles you can put on a leased car without incurring a penalty.

Money factor: Used to determine finance charges. This is usually negotiable—it should not be greater than the rate on loans. Money factor = [annual interest rate ÷ 24]

MSRP: Manufacturer's Suggested Retail Price. This is almost always negotiable (except on Saturn vehicles).

Open-end lease: Customer assumes risk for excess depreciation, might have to buy vehicle for more than it's worth, or sell at a loss and pay the leasing company the difference. (Very risky—avoid this type.)

Purchase option price: The amount that you can buy the vehicle for at the end of the lease. It's usually the same as the residual and it is negotiable.

Residual value: The estimated wholesale value of the vehicle at the end of the lease; used to calculate lease payments. (A higher residual should result in lower payments.) It's usually the same as the purchase option price, and it is negotiable.

Subsidized lease: An automaker's lease with an inflated residual and/or reduced interest rate that results in lower monthly payments.

Term: Length of lease. Don't lease longer than 3 years, or excess wear-and-tear charges could be expensive.

2

Buyer Beware:
Leasing Tricks & Scams

As the founder of a large lease-training company once said, *there is an opportunity to take advantage of the customer in a lease.* Since poorly-written consumer finance regulations did not require disclosure of important lease information (including the vehicle price or the interest rate), leasing companies and dealers didn't provide it. This gave unscrupulous salesmen a great opportunity to commit outrageous acts of fraud with little chance of being discovered. Or so they thought.

While the number of people leasing was growing in leaps and bounds, the volume of consumer complaints was also picking up steam. At first, it appeared to be just a few isolated stories of people who said they were misled and cheated on lease transactions, but it soon began to look like a more serious problem.

By 1992, some consumer protection agencies were beginning to get hundreds of complaints about new-car leasing, which led to the formation of a task force by the attorneys general from 22 states. A number of investigations were started, and dozens of lawsuits have been filed.

What were the complaints about? Many of them were about salesmen who had secretly raised the price of a car (or the APR on a loan) after quoting a lower one. And some people said they received no credit for their trade-ins, while others received less than the amount that was negotiated. Similarly, down payments and rebates were often not properly credited. (In some cases, salesmen had secretly increased the cap cost to cancel out the effect of trade-ins and down payments.) A common complaint of elderly buyers was that they were switched to leases without their knowledge.

The following investigations and lawsuits illustrate the numerous ways that people have been victimized by leasing scams. In all of the legal cases, most of the victims did not even realize they had been cheated.

PrimeTime Live Investigation

In a February, 1995 broadcast of ABC's *PrimeTime Live*, a hidden camera revealed what had happened to several female "buyers" when they went shopping for new cars. Out of ten dealers that were visited, five tried to talk the shoppers into leasing instead of buying.

The undercover shoppers were offered deals that sounded good—lower monthly payments, lower interest rates, and less money down. But when the leasing deals were analyzed by experts, attempted overcharges were discovered in all of them.

At one dealer, the shopper was told that the interest rate on a loan would be 10.5%, but the salesman said he could get her a 3% rate on a lease. When the lease numbers were analyzed, the actual rate was 8.4% (which wasn't disclosed verbally or in the contract). Attempted overcharge: $2,100. A second dealer tried the same trick: he told her the rate on a loan was 7.75% compared to 3% on a lease, then wrote up her lease based on 7.4% (again, no disclosure). Attempted overcharge: $2,600.

Two other tricks were attempted by salesmen to get more money out of the *PrimeTime* shoppers: the "secret price boost" and the "disappearing trade-in." When one of the shoppers asked about purchasing a car that was advertised for $23,999 the salesman tried to talk her into a lease, then wrote up the leasing contract based on a price that was about $3,000 higher. Of course, the higher price wasn't disclosed in the contract.

The "disappearing trade-in" trick was used by two salesmen on the *PrimeTime* shoppers. At one dealer, the shopper was offered $6,000 for her trade-in, but the salesman told her that she would be better off if the trade-in wasn't put in writing. (He said that would lower the sales tax she paid, but no state charges tax on a trade-in.) Then the shopper agreed to put an additional $1,000 down, and the attempted overcharge got worse: her lease payment was quoted as $364 when it should have been only $153. (The trade-in and cash were not properly applied to the lease.) Total attempted overcharge: $7,500.

A second salesman also tried the "disappearing trade-in" trick on a *PrimeTime* shopper. After negotiating a lower price on a new vehicle, the shopper was promised $10,000 for her trade-in. However, the lease payment quoted for that transaction was $389 when it should have been $193. (Only $5,800 had been credited for her trade-in, not the $10,000 that was promised.) Total attempted overcharge: $7,000.

The 10 visits to dealers by *PrimeTime* shoppers resulted in 5 attempts to put them in leases containing overcharges totaling $26,400. In addition to the undercover incidents, *PrimeTime* also included interviews with people who had recently leased new cars and claimed that similar things had happened to them.

Florida Investigations

According to Florida Attorney General Bob Butterworth, leasing fraud is a national problem. His office conducted a 2-year investigation of 26,000 auto leases, finding flagrant examples of fraud in about 10%. A few of the offenses: inflating price stickers used to determine lease payments, manipulating customers into leasing instead of buying, pocketing trade-in money instead of applying it to the lease, and under-valued trade-ins. Some people who signed leases thought they were buying their cars.

One of the attorney general's investigations targeted the leasing practices of that state's Toyota dealers, and a settlement was announced in May of 1995. Southeast Toyota Distributors Inc. and 55 Florida Toyota dealers agreed to set up a $4.5 million restitution fund to settle complaints regarding past leasing practices.

The Toyota dealers were accused of overcharging their customers, and the average amount of restitution was about $1,500. Some consumers received several thousand dollars.

California Investigations

A 1995-96 investigation by the Sacramento County District Attorney resulted in charges against five local Ford dealers. The dealers were accused of overcharging lease customers by inflating the early-payoff amounts on cars and trucks that were leased through Ford Motor Credit.

To settle the charges, all five dealers agreed to pay civil penalties (from $2,500 to $87,500 each) and make restitution to affected customers. A total of 111 people were entitled to restitution, with some receiving as much as $2,000. (This is believed to be a widespread practice. See Chapter 3 for more information on Ford leasing practices.)

Mazda Sued for Deceptive Lease Ads

In October of 1996, the attorneys general from 14 states filed lawsuits against Mazda Motor Corp. of America, charging the company with running lease ads that were misleading and deceptive. According to the California attorney general, the company's ads were misleading the public into thinking that they could lease a car with no money down, when they could not.

The ads in question claimed that people could lease a new Mazda for "zero down" or "one penny down," but customers were required to pay up-front money for acquisition fees, a refundable security deposit, the first month's payment, taxes, and license fees. The total up-front fees were usually in excess of $850.

According to the lawsuits, disclaimers for Mazda's television ads appeared at the bottom of the screen in tiny type, using uncommon abbreviations, and were only on the screen for a very short period of time, making it impossible for consumers to read and understand them.

The attorneys general also said that Mazda's internal documents showed that those types of ads were aimed at attracting consumers who would normally be hesitant about "out-of-pocket" spending.

In December, Mazda settled the charges by agreeing

to change its advertising practices. The company also agreed to pay $857,500 for costs of the investigation.

FTC Investigation: Deceptive Advertising

In 1996, five automakers were charged by the Federal Trade Commission with using deceptive advertising to market leases. General Motors, Mitsubishi Motor Sales of America, Mazda Motor of America, American Isuzu Motors, and American Honda Motor Co. were all accused of not providing proper disclosure in their television ads, making it difficult for consumers to determine the actual costs involved in the advertised deals.

For the most part, the companies' advertisements had provided disclosure, but they were not in readable type. Mazda, Honda, and Mitsubishi advertised "zero-down" leases, using fine-print disclaimers that mentioned up-front costs that customers were required to pay. Ads run by General Motors and Mitsubishi had final balloon payment amounts in unreadable type.

Similar charges had been filed against the five companies by attorneys general from 23 states. Initially, four of the companies agreed to settle the charges by changing their advertising practices. Mazda did not agree to settle until after 14 states filed lawsuits.

Class-Action Lawsuits

In over a dozen class-action lawsuits, leasing companies have been accused of violating consumer lending laws by charging excessive early-termination penalties on leases. According to plaintiffs' attorneys, leasing companies are not allowed to collect more than three times the monthly payment as a penalty. In many cases, companies were making their customers pay penalties of $4,000 to $5,000 (or more), even though the monthly payments were only $300 to $400.

At the time this book was being completed, one of these lawsuits was pending against Ford Motor Credit Co. The original attorney for the plaintiffs had reached a settlement with Ford that appeared to limit the company's total liability to well under $1 million, with the maximum number of eligible claimants limited to 100,000.

Even though the suit only pertained to Ford's early termination practices, the settlement appeared to protect the company—and its dealers—from any other claims or damages related to their leasing practices, by consumers who had previously entered into leases with Ford Motor Credit.

Another law firm (with a similar suit) filed court papers objecting to the proposed settlement, saying that it was unenforceable because it attempted to waive consumers' rights to recover damages suffered as a result of intentional, dishonest sales practices at Ford dealers.

Attorneys general from seven states also filed objections to the settlement, stating that it was unfair and inadequate because of its limits on restitution and its release of Ford against any other claims regarding its leasing practices. They also said that there were considerably more than one million potential claimants involved, and told the court that leasing abuses have victimized many who are unaware that they were cheated. After hearing the objections, the judge did not approve the settlement.

LEASING TRICKS, SCAMS, & LIES

The following leasing tricks, scams, and lies have been widely used by dishonest car salesmen to cheat their customers. Should you experience any of these, assume that you are dealing with an unethical salesman, then find a more honest dealership for your business. If you think their practices were really dishonest, file a complaint with the consumer protection divisions of your state attorney general and local district attorney.

On the other hand, if you spend a lot of time discussing leases with a particular dealer and they don't use any of these tricks, they're probably honest. The honest ones deserve your business, not the other guys. And tell your friends, too.

The phony lease-versus-buy comparison. To make lease payments look more attractive, the salesman compares them to loan payments that are based on a shorter term than most buyers typically choose. (Most buyers choose 5-year loans, but salesmen often use 3-4 year loans in their comparison because the payments are higher.) Also, the higher costs of car insurance and registration fees related to short-term leasing are conveniently left out.

The "down payment" trick. Down payments are often used in leasing to make a bad deal look good. On a lease, a down payment is just monthly (rental) payments in advance, it doesn't reduce the residual or purchase option price. Salesmen often equate down payments on leases with down payments on purchases, but only on purchases do they build any equity.

There is no purchase price on a lease. This dishonest statement has been used by many salesmen after their customers asked, "What price am I paying for this car?" The purpose: to prevent disclosing the cap cost and to hide secret price increases.

The secret price boost. After you negotiate a lower purchase price on a vehicle, the salesman switches you to a lease with a higher cap cost than the negotiated price. (This is known in the industry as "the flip," and salesmen have been offered bonuses to flip buyers into leases.)

The cap cost has no effect on your payment. Another dishonest statement that's been used by salesmen after they were caught using higher cap costs than the prices that were previously negotiated (or quoted).

There is no interest rate on a lease. This dishonest statement is used to hide the actual interest rate being charged on a lease. (No rate disclosure in the contract.)

The secret APR boost. The salesman quotes you a lower interest rate for a lease, then writes up the contract based on a higher rate. Since there's no rate disclosure in the lease contract, you don't know it's been increased.

The disappearing trade-in. After negotiating a price on your trade-in, the salesman fails to credit the full amount in the lease—or he just increases the cap cost to cancel out part of the trade-in. (Sometimes none of the trade-in amount is credited. This is known as a "home run.")

The disappearing (cash) down payment. After talking you into putting additional cash down (to lower your monthly payments), the salesman fails to credit the full amount in the lease—or he just increases the cap cost to cancel out part of the down payment. (Sometimes none of the cap reduction is credited. This is also known as a "home run.")

You don't pay for the whole car, only the part you use. This dishonest statement is used to convince you that leasing is cheaper than buying. The salesman fails to mention that you will be paying interest on the whole car (not just "the part you use"), and the total interest you pay on a lease will be a lot higher than it would be on a loan at the same terms.

"No money down" advertising. Ads say that you can lease with no down payment, but lease companies almost always require the first month's payment and a security deposit, in addition to tax, license, and registration fees.

The future value of the vehicle is guaranteed. This little trick is often used to hide the fact that the residual (or purchase option price) has been inflated. In other words, the vehicle will be worth less (sometimes a lot less) than the residual at the end of the lease.

Deceptive advertising. Low-payment ads are run for leases that require large down payments and/or trade-ins. Also, advertised prices are often limited to one vehicle, or they only apply to stripped-down models.

The phony "investment earnings" claim. Salesmen often use hypothetical investment earnings on the "initial cash savings from a lease" to make it look better. Since so many people who lease low-to-mid-priced vehicles are leasing because they can't afford higher loan payments, the "investment earnings" claim is phony because most people won't have anything "left over" to invest.

The dishonest "financing is cheaper" program. Some salesmen have talked all-cash buyers into leasing after using a dishonest computer program to "prove" that financing is cheaper than paying cash. *It isn't.* (About 5,000 dealers in the U.S. purchased this program.) Even when below-market financing is available, it's almost always offered instead of a (cash) customer rebate, so it might only be a bargain if you intend to borrow a lot for a long time (which isn't smart, anyway).

Inadequate disclosure. Failing to disclose any of the following in writing: cap cost (purchase price), cap reduction, trade-in, residual, monthly payment, total finance charges, interest rate, allowable mileage, excess mileage charge, acquisition and disposition fees (if any), total due at lease signing, purchase option price, and explanation of termination penalty.

NOTE TO LEASE VICTIMS

If you think that you were victimized by any of the tricks described in this chapter, be sure to read "Note to Victims of Leasing Fraud" on the Summary page. It will explain what you should do if fraud was involved to cheat you on a lease.

Leasing Lessons for Smart Shoppers

3

Ford's Success Story:
Was It Leasing or Fleecing?

As the first automaker to heavily promote short-term leasing, Ford quickly became the industry leader in leases as a percentage of new-car sales. After seeing Ford's profits and market share increase using that strategy, other companies decided to jump on the leasing bandwagon.

However, Ford's "brilliant marketing strategy" may not deserve all the credit for the dramatic increase in short-term leases that occurred in their dealer network between 1989 and 1995. In fact, Ford had set up (or tolerated) a number of practices that would entice its dealers to write a lot more leases. Of course, those practices all involved opportunities for Ford's dealers and salespeople to make a lot more money on leases than they would on purchases. Unfortunately for their customers, those huge profits were often made by tricking people into leases that involved overcharging and other fraudulent acts.

To be fair, I must state that the following unethical practices were not necessarily being used by all Ford and Lincoln-Mercury dealers and/or their salespeople. For example, in the "payoff-packing" scheme, only five Ford dealers (out of eight in that area) were charged with inflating payoff amounts to cheat their customers. And some sales/finance staff refused to carry out the deceptive tricks that were taught in the national training program, as evidenced by their demotions and terminations.

Some of the unethical practices that existed in the Ford Motor Credit lease program include: concealing payoff amounts from customers, ignoring outrageous acts of overcharging by its dealers, refusing to provide cap cost and APR disclosure in its lease contracts (which allowed overcharges and fraud to occur), recommending and/or providing a national training program that taught deceptive (and fraudulent) sales techniques, and paying secret bonuses to salespeople for recommending a lease over a purchase.

The following sections describe how those practices were set up, carried out, and/or tolerated by Ford, and how their lease customers were often cheated as a direct result of those practices.

Concealing Payoff Amounts from Customers (The "Payoff-Packing" Scheme)

Three former employees of a Florida Lincoln-Mercury dealer (from 1989-91) described a "payoff-packing" scheme that was used to overcharge customers who had leased through Ford Motor Credit. They said that representatives from Ford Credit told them how to inflate customers' early-payoff amounts, explaining that their Ford Credit branch would "participate" by refusing to give payoff amounts to customers who requested them. Instead, they were told that customers would be referred back to the dealer for payoff information, giving them "an opportunity to make additional profits" by overcharging their customers.

According to a former finance manager, Ford Credit would only reveal payoff amounts to managers who were "approved" by Ford. And dealers were instructed to keep a logbook to record payoff balances that were given to customers, so they wouldn't be caught giving out different numbers.

Two of the former employees said that Ford Credit representatives used this "payoff-packing opportunity" as a marketing tool to entice dealers to give Ford most (or all) of their leasing business.

Five years later, in California, the Sacramento County District Attorney's office received a complaint of overcharging on a lease payoff by a local Ford dealer. Investigators discovered that Ford Credit had been concealing payoff information from their lease customers, so the investigation was expanded to include all early payoffs that occurred at that one dealer over a one-year period. It was discovered that 31 people had been overcharged.

That 1995 investigation of one Ford dealer quickly spread to include eight Ford dealers in that area. When it was over, five of the dealers were accused of overcharging their customers by inflating the early-payoff amounts on cars and trucks that were leased through Ford Motor Credit. (And the district attorney's office said they found logbooks that were used to keep track of amounts that were quoted to customers.)

To settle the charges, all five dealers agreed to pay

civil penalties (from $2,500 to $87,500 each) and make restitution to affected customers. A total of 111 people were entitled to restitution, with some receiving as much as $2,000. (The Sacramento investigation only covered payoffs that occurred during a 12-month period, which turned up 111 victims.) Similar investigations were then started by district attorneys in other areas.

"Payoff packing" is believed to have been a common practice at a number of Ford and Lincoln-Mercury dealers, since Ford Motor Credit was the only lender to withhold payoff information from its lease customers. (My sources estimate that this scheme was being used by as many as 65-70% of the Ford and Lincoln-Mercury dealers.)

The company stopped concealing lease payoffs in late 1995 after the investigations were started.

Outrageous Overcharging Ignored

Ford Motor Credit witnessed outrageous acts of overcharging by its dealers and did nothing to stop them. In some cases, vehicle prices had been secretly increased by $5,000 (or more) over suggested retail and Ford Credit approved the leases, collected the money from customers, and paid the dealers their "share" of the profits.

For example, Florida resident Carla Higginbotham leased a 1994 Ford Mustang through Ford Credit, making a cash down payment of $4,695. Since the price was not disclosed in the lease, the dealer was able to increase it to $25,692—a secret "bump" to $4,802 above MSRP. As the result of that "disappearing down payment" trick, her monthly payment was $441 when it should have been $250.

(By the way, when Higginbotham was asked why she made such a large down payment on a lease, she said she thought it was a purchase, not a lease. For more on this common "misunderstanding," see "deceptive sales practices" later in this chapter.)

A similar thing happened to W.E. Mulkey in Georgia, who leased a 1994 Ford Ranger through Ford Credit. He made a down payment of $6,319 which should have reduced his monthly payment to about $3 (yes, that's right: only three dollars), but he was charged $251 per month for the whole term. The price of his vehicle had been secretly increased by $5,500 over MSRP. (Out of eight leases involved in one lawsuit against Ford over early termination, six of them had overcharges ranging from $1,175 to $5,500.)

Several attorneys general working on leasing investigations say that fraud is assumed to be involved any time a vehicle price is increased by more than 5% above retail. In those two examples, the increases were 22% above retail for Higginbotham, and 36% above retail for Mulkey. And Ford Credit has been well aware of outrageous overcharges such as those two, because they receive itemized reports from dealers that contain the information.

Dealers were required to complete a "dealer worksheet" for every lease that was turned in to Ford Credit, listing the actual selling price, the suggested retail price, and the exact amount of mark-up on the vehicle. Any price increases that occurred would have been immediately noticeable on the worksheets. For example, the dealer worksheet for the Higginbotham lease showed the $4,802 price increase, and listed the total mark-up as $6,388—on a car that retailed for $20,890. (The normal dealer mark-up on a car in that price range would be about $2,000.)

Ford even had a system set up to handle significant overcharges. In their Red Carpet Lease (RCL) dealer handbook, under "Excess Deferred Gross," dealers were told that the company would withhold funds from the dealer on leases that had "excess mark-up." At the end of the lease, Ford Credit would then pay the rest of the money to the dealer—but only if the car was purchased by the customer or dealer, not if it was turned in to Ford.

Apparently it was OK for dealers to take advantage of their customers, but cheating Ford would not be tolerated. The company's dealer handbook said, "Ford Credit does not restrict the amount of profit the dealer may include in a lease, only how much is advanced to the dealer at lease inception."

Refused to Disclose Cap Cost or APR
In Spite of Overcharging & Fraud

Since the law did not require written disclosure of cap costs or interest rates, Ford Motor Credit did not provide it. This allowed its dealers to use (and get away with) deceptive sales practices, such as quoting lower prices and interest rates than people actually received. And it allowed dealers to overcharge their customers. (There's evidence that dealers were trained to do this. See "deceptive sales practices" later in this chapter.)

Even after witnessing numerous acts of blatant overcharging (from dealer worksheets), Ford did not provide disclosure of cap costs until July of 1995, following an investigation in Florida. At the time of publication, the company was still not providing written disclosure of interest rates to its lease customers.

Deceptive Interest Rate Quotes

Ford's method of calculating and quoting interest rates on leases allowed its dealers to deceive their customers into thinking that they were getting lower rates. And since the company did not provide written disclosure of the actual rates, dealers were free to quote any rate that sounded good, without fear of getting caught.

In many cases, the actual interest rates on Ford leases were about 1.5 to 2.0 points higher than those charged by other lenders. Quoting lower rates obviously helped dealers to convince people that their leases were "good deals," even though the rates may have been deceptive. (Recent quotes obtained from a number of Ford dealers understated the actual interest rates by about $30 a month on one particular vehicle.)

Ford's "rate discrepancy" is due to a hidden administrative fee that the company adds to its monthly finance charges, but only the "base rate" is used when quoting rates to customers. The undisclosed part of the finance charges causes the real APR to be a lot higher, so if a dealer tells you the "rate" on a lease is 9.0%, it's probably closer to 10.75%.

The company's RCL dealer handbook explained this hidden fee in a question-and-answer section: "Q: Is a lease factor like 10.50 the same as a 10.50% APR? A: No. The lease monthly payment may include local fees, where applicable, and an administrative fee of 1/9 of 1% of the acquisition cost. *The implicit rate to the customer is approximately 1.75% point higher than the stated factor.*" [emphasis mine]

Secret Kickbacks to Dealers for Inflating Rates

According to Ford's RCL dealer handbook, dealers were offered extra money for writing leases with interest rates that were above their standard lease factors: "The dealer shares up front with Ford Credit additional lease income earned over the lease term as follows: Lease Term 24 (Months), Dealer Portion 85%/Lease Term 36 (Months), Dealer Portion 75%/Lease Term 48 (Months), Dealer

Portion 65%."

Since Ford provided no written disclosure of interest rates on its leases, their customers would have had no idea that dealers were increasing their rates. Obviously, dealers would not have mentioned it to their customers when it was being done. So a dealer who secretly raised the rate on a lease by two points would receive additional income of $675 for increasing a customer's total finance charges by $900.

This practice appears to be illegal, because someone acting as a loan "broker" (i.e., someone who is compensated for arranging and placing loans) must provide disclosure to customers when they are being paid by lenders for placing loans with them. And that's clearly not being done by Ford Credit or its dealers.

This is a very common practice in the car business; most lenders pay dealers for giving them loan or lease business. (Without disclosure, of course.) Unfortunately for consumers, it often results in customers getting stuck with lenders who offer bigger kickbacks, not lower rates.

Secret Bonuses to Salespeople for Leases

An article in *Automotive News* told how Ford had been offering cash bonuses to its salespeople for writing Red Carpet Leases. Typical bonus amounts were $75 to $100 per lease, but the bonus was increased if the new lease was a renewal. Some bonuses were as high as $500 per vehicle, and this was in addition to their normal salary and/or commission. The bonus program was started in 1989 and was supposedly discontinued in 1995.

So Ford's salespeople were presenting themselves to customers as "trusted advisors" and telling them that leasing was the smart thing to do, while they were being paid generous bonuses for convincing people to lease. (And they still got bonuses, and bigger commission checks, if they overcharged customers on leases.) Of course, their customers weren't told about the bonuses, or the fact that so many of them had been overcharged.

FORD'S NATIONAL LEASE TRAINING

Deceptive Sales Practices Taught

To train salespeople regarding Ford's Red Carpet Leases, the company recommended and/or provided national training seminars through Half-A-Car, Inc. since 1986. (Half-A-Car is an independent company that provides lease training exclusively for Ford.)

In sworn statements and trial testimony, former salespeople described the training program as teaching the use of lies, deception, and fraud to trick customers into leases that involved overcharges. They also said that when they objected to what they described as "criminal activity," they were terminated, slandered, and blackballed from the car business.

In a December 17, 1994 interview in *The Palm Beach Post,* Assistant Attorney General Jack Norris of Florida said this after being shown the Half-A-Car training manual: "On its face, it's an instruction book on how to build a facade to avoid disclosing that the deal is a lease. It's deceptive." Last year, another state's assistant attorney general said he thought their training manual was "actionable." (In other words, he thought it violated the law regarding deceptive business practices.)

In *The Palm Beach Post* article, the founder of Half-A-Car denied that his seminars taught improper sales techniques. He said, "There is an opportunity to take advantage of the customer in a lease because the focus is on (monthly) payments, not price. But we teach our dealers not to do something that is going to hurt them down the road." In another *Palm Beach Post* article about Ford's lease training, a Ford spokesman said, "There's no intent for it to be deceptive."

Was Ford's national lease training program deceptive, as the salesmen and prosecutors claimed? Or were Ford and their training company correct in claiming that it was not? And if the training was deceptive, did Ford know about it?

To address the last question first, Ford actively promoted the Half-A-Car training: All dealers were expected to participate by sending their employees to the seminars and installing the program in their dealerships as soon as their personnel had completed the training. According to sworn statements and court testimony, salesmen who refused to go along were often branded as troublemakers who lost their jobs.

One seminar attendee said he was told by the Half-A-Car instructor, during the first hour of a 1990 training seminar, "The senior vice president of Ford Motor Credit attended this same presentation two months earlier." And an affidavit from a former salesman mentioned the training being held in Ford's conference room. With all the pressure on dealers to "participate" in the training, it's hard to believe that Ford didn't know what their dealers were being taught.

To discover what was actually being taught in those seminars, I decided to track down the training materials that were used by Half-A-Car. I ended up with three complete training manuals that were used between 1989 and 1995, plus a Ford Red Carpet Lease Dealer Handbook. I also found a number of sworn statements from seminar attendees who testified in court cases regarding Ford's lease training and sales practices.

The training materials from the Half-A-Car manuals, along with interviews and sworn statements, show that Ford's national lease training was, in fact, extremely deceptive. Key parts of their training are explained in the following sections, which include numerous quotes from actual training materials that illustrate the deception.

To avoid repetition, only one manual will be referenced at a time. There is no significant difference between the 1989 and 1993 manuals—the same deceptive practices are taught in both.

Hiding the Truth: It's a Lease, Not a Purchase

In affidavits and depositions, former salespeople said that they were taught to deceive customers by Half-A-Car. In a sworn statement, one of them said, "We were taught that we should disguise the important fact that 'The Plan' is a lease, because leasing terms were said to be a 'turnoff' to customers. We were provided with a misleading list of words used to describe a retail sale and we were ordered to use those words instead. We were told that this was to conceal from our customer the fact that the transaction was indeed a lease. Even the name of 'The Plan' was part of this deception."

Documents from the training manuals show that Ford dealers and salespeople were, in fact, given sales material and training that enabled them to deceive customers into thinking that they were purchasing, when they were being set up to sign lease contracts. Instead of using words that would indicate a lease, they were trained to use terms that sounded like a purchase.

Page 7 of the 1989 manual says, "When we mention the word 'lease', people don't think of the third alternative. They think of 'old' leasing, and they don't want any part of that. They would prefer to buy. Because of this think-

41

ing, leasing terms are 'turn-off' words. We need to be able to describe all of the benefits of the third alternative without the use of 'turn-off' leasing terms. Buying terms won't turn the customer off—so we should use them instead." The following lists appeared on the same page, under "Buying Language." The left side was preprinted, and the instructor provided the terms on the right.

GET RID OF:	REPLACE WITH:
Lease	The Plan
Buy	To Get
Capitalized Cost	Selling Price
Capitalized Cost Reduction	Down Payment
Acquisition Cost	Balance to Finance
Residual	Guaranteed Future Value
Interest Rate	Cost of Funds

The word "lease" did not appear in numerous worksheets and sales aids that were supposed to be used with customers. Instead, it was referred to as "The Plan" or "The Half-A-Car Plan." The following words were used frequently in worksheets and other sales aids: "ownership, equity, you don't owe anything, guaranteed future value, keep it, trade or sell, keep the profit, you own..."

One worksheet appeared a number of times in the manuals, and blanks were provided for dealers to use with customers (page 3-35 in the 1989 manual). It was titled, "Comparison Example" and it contained a number of deceptions. On this worksheet under the "Half-A-Car Way" it says, "Two Years Later..You Don't Owe Anything, You Own 3 Options... Option 1. Trade or Sell, The Joy of New, (Keep the Profit)...[Option] 3. Keep It..." Nowhere on the page was the word "lease" mentioned.

Another worksheet (page 3-6 in the 1993 manual) says, "Good news Mr. Customer...Your monthly pay-

ments are only $_____ for only 24 months And at the
end of the two years you would have a paid-up contract
And you own those three options at the bottom...3 Options You Own: 1. Trade, Sell, Profit!...2. What If?
Avoid Loss...3. Keep It!!! Ownership." Blank copies of
this form were also included for use with customers (page
3-9 in the 1989 manual). No mention is made of the fact
that it's a lease.

Other worksheets and sales aids with the same deceptive terms appear in the manuals, some teaching strategies
and tricks aimed at convincing customers that Ford's Plan
provided ownership, without disclosing that it was really
just a lease.

If someone asked whether The Plan was a lease, the
salespeople were told to say, "They took the best parts of
conventional financing (ownership and equity) and only
the best parts of a lease, and formed this new program
called [The Plan]." That instruction was on page 7a in
the 1989 manual, under "Lease Disclosure." (In the 1993
manual, that instruction was supposedly changed, replac-
ing "program" with "3rd generation lease.")

So the training program equipped salespeople to convince the public that Ford's lease program was something
special. Salespeople were taught to refer to it as "a new
program," "The Plan," and "The Half-A-Car Way."

The truth is that there was nothing special at all about
Ford's "Plan," except for the dishonest way that it was to
be presented to customers. The Half-A-Car Plan was
really nothing more than a typical, garden-variety, short-
term lease with a purchase option. It didn't provide "ownership" for anyone (without making a huge balloon payment), and it didn't provide real "equity" for over 95% of
those who leased.

Those who signed papers without reading them may
not have seen (or heard) the word "lease" until much lat-

er. Because they trusted the dealer, they ignored the lease words in the final contract—after all, the dealer said they could keep the car at the end of the contract.

This explains why a number of people were tricked into making huge down payments on leases, which they never would have done if they had been told that they wouldn't get to keep the car at the end of the contract. As mentioned earlier, Carla Higginbotham said that she was tricked into a lease. When she made a down payment of $4,695 on a new Mustang, she thought it was a purchase.

In a *Palm Beach Post* article, Samuel Kountz of Florida said he thought he was buying his new Mercury under a new Ford "plan." In a complaint he filed against the dealer, he said, "Nobody uttered the word 'lease' to us." He claimed that he was tricked into signing a lease: "I felt like a fool. I certainly would not have added $1,500 worth of options to a car that was not mine."

And in trial testimony for a Florida lawsuit, a number of people claimed—under oath—that they were tricked into signing leases. They said the word "lease" was never mentioned by salespeople.

Concealing Prices from Customers

The training seminars also taught salespeople to focus customers on monthly payments and avoid discussing or disclosing the cap costs of vehicles. Numerous strategies and tricks were taught that were designed to conceal the actual prices that customers were paying.

For example, page 3-30 of the 1989 manual says, "Customer Response: What are you charging me for the car?" It then explains how to deceive the customer into thinking the deal has a big discount: "Salesperson: Mr. Customer, are asking me what kind of a discount you are getting?" Salespeople were then taught a deceptive strategy: to add up the monthly payments (and any down payment) on the lease, comparing the total with the MSRP to trick customers into thinking that the price was a lot lower than suggested retail.

No mention was made of revealing the actual price (or cap cost). And that was important, since dealers and salespeople were also taught how to cheat customers on discounts and secretly increase the prices of cars.

Cheating Customers on Discounts

Ford's lease training included instruction on how to misquote monthly payments to cheat customers out of negotiated discounts. If a customer said that he would not OK a deal unless they gave him a price discount on a car, they were taught how to trick him into believing that a smaller payment reduction was legitimate.

A number of documents in the training manuals told salespeople that the proper monthly payment change for each $1,000 in gross [price] was $50. Page 2-30 in the 1993 manual says, "Rule! $1,000 in Gross = $50 in Payment. We can simplify by using a 'rule of thumb' Factor of 2." And page 2-34 in the same manual says, "We know that $60 in payments is equal to $1,200 in Gross." It also mentioned the "Factor of 2."

However, on a page titled, "What Kind of Discount Are You Giving Me?" (3-9 in the 1993 manual), salespeople were told to use a different factor to figure payment reductions for discounts. The manual tells how to do this in front of the customer: "Write down the discount amount, then using a "3" factor, convert that to a lower payment amount: — $1,500 discount equals $45 per month."

Since the monthly payment reduction they were quoting (for 2 years) was about the same as the real one on a

3-year loan, most people would not have known that they were being cheated out of 40% of their discount.

Secret Price Increases & Stolen Down Payments

In affidavits and trial testimony, former salesmen said Half-A-Car taught them how to secretly increase prices to "steal" customers' down payments, rebates, and trade-in equity. (And since they had already been taught how to conceal the prices from customers, that would be an easy trick to pull off.)

Notes taken during a 1990 Half-A-Car seminar quote the instructor as saying, "If you limit the price increase (bump) to $2,500 the customer is unlikely to catch it, even if he tries to re-calculate the figures or car price on his own." He was then asked what the dealership liability would be if a customer found out that they had secretly raised the price of a car. According to the notes, his response was, "Legally or ethically?" Another salesman added, "Ethically? We're not being ethical to start with!"

Salespeople were told that down payments on leases would lower monthly payments for customers, while providing higher gross profits for dealers (page 27a in the 1989 manual). They were then taught to talk customers into making larger down payments when they complained that monthly payments were too high.

On page 2-46 of the 1989 manual, an exercise is used to show how to get the same gross profit out of a customer who says the payments are too high. Instead of $1,000 down and $400 a month (for 24 months), the manual shows that getting $2,500 down will provide the same gross for the dealer, even though the new lease payment is only $325 a month.

This trick could be used to secretly increase prices on cars. Since most people know that it's smart to make a larger down payment on a conventional loan, deceiving customers into paying higher (undisclosed) prices using the "down payment trick" would have been easy to accomplish. (Down payments on leases are simply monthly payments paid in advance. The residual or purchase option price at the end of a lease will be the same, regardless of whether the customer makes a down payment of $5 or $5,000.)

To aid in this deception, salespeople were taught how to use dishonest "Comparison Example" worksheets, as explained in the following section.

Deceptive Lease-versus-Buy Comparisons

To convince people that The Plan was a smart thing to do, salespeople were taught how to deceive them using "Comparison Example" worksheets. They were told to tell customers, "Mr. Customer—The arithmetic of the [Plan] is just like the arithmetic of buying." (page 43 of the 1989 manual) "You have the same selling price...The same down payment...The same balance..." *The word "lease" did not appear on the worksheet.*

That statement about the "arithmetic" of The Plan was completely dishonest—down payments on leases do not have the same financial effect as down payments on purchases. On a lease, the "final payoff" amount necessary to keep a car is the residual, and that number is completely unaffected by down payments. That is not the case in a conventional loan transaction.

Half-A-Car's training for the "Comparison Example" involved several major deceptions. First, salespeople were told "Always compare 48 month retail to 24 month Plan." (1993 manual, page 2-14) This was done to make conventional loan payments look higher than The Plan. (The most commonly-used loan term is 60 months, and quoting those lower payments would have made The Plan's payments far less attractive.)

Monthly payments on a lease should be a lot lower than payments on a loan, since less principal (equity) is being paid off during the whole term. However, Ford salespeople were taught to quote Plan payments that were only a little lower than 48-month loan payments. This was done to secretly raise the effective price of the car to a higher amount than the one shown on the worksheet— and no one would ever notice.

According to salesmen who attended the training, they were taught how to use the "Comparison Example" worksheets to secretly inflate prices and steal customers' down payments. Notes taken during a training seminar show exactly how this was done, using the worksheet on page 4-2 of the 1989 manual.

The instructor told them to use the same selling price, down payment, and balance on both sides of the work-sheet—under "Conventional" and "Half-A-Car Way." Then they were told to write down the conventional loan payment on the left, showing a payment on the right for the Half-A-Car Plan that was about $50 lower. However, the payment on the Plan side was actually the proper payment for a "zero-down" lease, so the cap cost was being secretly increased to cancel out the effect of the down payment.

What they had been taught was a perfect example of the "disappearing down payment" trick. And since they were being taught to lie about the selling price, they were teaching salespeople to commit fraud.

The third major deception that was taught using the comparison worksheet involved the balance due on a 48-month loan at the end of two years. On page 43 of the 1989 manual, salespeople were told to multiply the loan payment times 24 to show the customer how much he would owe on the conventional side (half-way through the loan), leading people to believe that the "bottom-line" numbers looked "better" on The Plan side.

That trick was completely dishonest, since the total that would result would include two years of future interest (i.e., the interest wouldn't really be owed at the midpoint of the loan). On a $20,000 loan at 8%, that trick would result in a lie that represents $916. (Of course, it's a lie that makes The Plan look better.)

Equity & Guaranteed Future Value Deceptions

As mentioned earlier, salespeople were told to avoid the use of leasing terms because they were "turn-off words." Instead of "residual," they were told to use "guaranteed future value." They were also taught to use the words "equity" and "ownership" to trick people into thinking that a deal was a purchase, when it was really a lease.

Half-A-Car taught salespeople to promote the concept of Ford's "Guaranteed Future Value" as something special, a valuable customer benefit that would provide equity at the end of the 2-year term. (1989 manual: pages 8, 2-25, 3-34) Customers were told that Ford would guarantee the future wholesale value of the car, including a very creative fabrication involving nonexistent insurance. On page 3-30 of the manual, salespeople are taught to say, "And it would also include the cost of the guaranteed resale insurance to protect the value of the car at the end."

To help convince people that they would have equity, salespeople were told to say that Plan customers "gain exclusive membership to our Resale Club. That means 120 days before your cycle date, someone from the dealership will call and ask one question. If we could sell your used car and give you some of the profit, would you consider selling it?" (1993 manual, page 1A-39)

All of those terms and promises were nothing but smoke. Very few people who lease (from Ford or anyone else) ever have "equity" at the end of a lease, because residuals are usually set higher than the actual wholesale values. Over 75% of all new-car leases end with the customer giving the car back to the dealer and not receiving any real money or credit towards another vehicle. Even in cases where a "credit" is given, it's usually just "funny money" that disappears in another lease containing overcharges.

The few exceptions involve leases that are a bad deal to begin with because the monthly payments are set outrageously high using a low residual. And in a few rare cases, some customers have ended up with a vehicle that's worth more than the residual because the lender accidentally set the residual too low. But that doesn't happen very often, and Ford knows it.

Customers are not told that the "Guaranteed Future Value" used in most Ford leases is based on an unrealistic estimate of future wholesale values, which means that there won't be any real equity at the end of a lease.

A recent article in *Automotive News* contained a good illustration of Ford's "inflated residuals." The article told of a pilot program at Ford's Lincoln-Mercury Division that allows dealers to purchase off-lease Lincolns for less than the residual amounts. According to *Automotive News* , late-model Lincolns were selling at auction for $1,000 to $5,000 below anticipated residual values, and the company wanted to keep the cars out of the auctions.

However, the article said that dealers weren't interested in buying off-lease vehicles from Lincoln because they could buy the same cars at auction for as much as $1,500 below the company's discounted price. A company official confirmed that their dealers preferred to buy through auctions.

What's interesting about this story is that it reveals how Ford (through its Lincoln-Mercury Division) had inflated residuals on these cars to the point that they began losing as much as $5,000 per car at auction. But it wasn't just done on Lincolns.

In fact, inflating residuals is a common practice in the leasing business to make monthly payments more attractive, and Ford does this on a regular basis (without disclosure, of course). I did a study of residual values set by Ford on a number of vehicles that were involved in lawsuits agaist the company, and I found many residuals that were inflated by over $1,000 per car.

While I was out "spying" recently, I asked salesmen at several Ford dealers why they didn't have very many off-lease Tauruses or Escorts for sale. (Several hundred thousand of them had just been leased and turned back in, so the dealers' lots should have been covered with those models.) The salesmen said that they usually don't keep those cars because they're not worth the residual amount at the end of the lease. They said the dealers usually turn them in to Ford and the cars end up at auction, where they can buy them for less than the residual amount.

Since these facts are concealed from Ford's customers, it is a deceptive practice. Unfortunately, many consumers have fallen for the "Guaranteed Future Value" and "equity" tricks.

CURRENT INVESTIGATIONS

According to a June 26, 1995 *Automotive News* article, attorneys general from Florida and Washington "are targeting Ford Motor Co.-endorsed trainer Half-A-Car after snagging huge settlements from dealers for deceptive leasing practices."

The article said that dealers were pointing fingers at

trainers. Doug Walsh, assistant attorney general in Washington, was quoted as saying, "When I confronted dealers about their misrepresentations they said, 'What's the problem? They (trainers) told us how to do it.'" Walsh added, "This doesn't excuse the dealer, the trainer, and it doesn't provide a defense for the manufacturer or dealer that hires the trainer."

The Washington State Attorney General's Office has reached settlements with several Ford dealers already. In a case against one dealer, 46 consumers received restitution in amounts ranging from $200 to $1,200 each, for a grand total of $28,088. Another dealer settled charges by agreeing to a settlement of $385,000 (of which $100,000 was suspended on condition of compliance with the terms of the settlement).

As of late 1996, Florida's Attorney General has mediated 63 consumer complaints that were made against 10 Ford and Lincoln-Mercury dealers. The dealers agreed to make restitution averaging $1,500 for each affected customer. According to a spokesman for the attorney general's office, "This is an ongoing investigation."

Other states are also believed to be investigating Ford dealers for various acts of deceptive leasing practices.

NOTE TO LEASE VICTIMS

If you think that you were victimized by any of the tricks described in this chapter, be sure to read "Note to Victims of Leasing Fraud" on the Summary page. It will explain what you should do if fraud was involved to cheat you on a lease.

4

How to Figure Lease Payments

The only way to be sure that you are getting a good deal is to know exactly how much the lease payments should be, based on your research of prices, residuals, and interest rates. This chapter will explain how lease payments are calculated, using worksheets from the Appendix.

There are two different ways you can calculate lease payments: use a computer program like Expert Lease Pro (see Chapter 8, under "Leasing Software") or you can use a calculator and note paper. The program is handy because it's faster, and it's got the latest retail, invoice, and residual numbers built in. But it's not a necessity; a calculator and note paper will work just fine.

The following procedure for calculating lease payments is based on the "constant-yield method," which is used by all major leasing companies except Ford Motor Credit. Ford uses a weird "two-factor" method that many of their own salespeople can't explain, so it's not likely that consumers would be able to obtain both factors to calculate their payments. (Expert Lease can calculate payments using Ford's method if you have both factors.)

My advice: If you're interested in leasing a Ford, just use the constant-yield method to figure out what the payments should be, then see how Ford's numbers measure up. If their payments look good, you might want to take their deal. If they're too high, tell the dealer to find another leasing company—or you'll find another dealer.

To calculate payments and total cost, we'll use the worksheets from the back of the book, displaying them right next to the explanations. Worksheet #1 organizes the information that we'll need, and Worksheet #2 runs the numbers through the formulas. First we'll figure payments on a lease with no cap reduction, then we'll do the same lease again with a $2,000 down payment.

Here's our first worksheet: The MSRP on the car is $22,000 but we negotiated the price down to $20,000. (That was easy!) We don't want to buy any extra insurance or warranties, so our gross cap cost (C) is still $20,000. There's no down payment, trade-in, or rebate, so our total cap cost reduction (G) is zero and the net cap cost (C minus G) is $20,000. It's a 3-year lease, so we enter the term as 36 months. The current rate on car loans is 8% and the residual is $11,000 (50% of MSRP). The acquisition fee is $450 and the title fees are $400 (estimated at 2% of the purchase price). We'll fill in the monthly payment and security deposit sections later, with the totals.

Now we're ready for Worksheet #2.

Worksheet #1 — Lease Information

Vehicle year, make, model ___*1997 LeaseMobile XLT*___

Retail price (MSRP) ___*22,000*___

Vehicle Price:

A. Negotiated vehicle price ___*20,000*___

B. Add-ons: (warranty, insurance, etc.)

_____

C. <u>Gross cap cost</u> (A+B)   ___*20,000*___

Credits:

D. Cash down payment   ___*0*___

E. Net trade-in allowance ___*0*___

F. Rebates   ___*0*___

G. <u>Total cap cost reduction</u> (D+E+F)   ___*0*___

Lease Terms:

<u>Net cap cost</u> (C minus G)   ___*20,000*___

Term _*36*_ Money factor _____ Interest rate _*8%*_

Monthly payment _____ Residual value _*11,000*_

H. <u>Total of monthly payments</u>   _____

Amounts due at lease signing:

Cash down payment (optional)   _____

Net trade-in allowance (optional)   _____

Refundable security deposit   _____

1) Acquisition fee   ___*450*___

2) Title/registration fees   ___*400*___

3) Sales tax on cap reduction (G)   _____

First month's payment   _____

<u>Total due at lease signing</u>   _____

Total cost of lease (G+H+1+2+3)   _____

In Worksheet #2, we use the net cap cost, residual, term, and interest rate from our Lease Information sheet.

Note: The residual you use will be provided by the dealer, but you should always check it against the one listed in the current *Automotive Lease Guide*. (See Chapter 8.) That way you'll know if the dealer's residual is too low or too high. If it's too low, your monthly payments will be higher. If it's been inflated, your monthly payments will be lower, but the car won't be worth the residual/purchase option price at the end of the lease.

<u>Part 1 calculates the monthly depreciation:</u> We subtract the residual ($11,000) from the net cap cost ($20,000) to get $9,000. Then we divide that by 36 (the number of months in the lease) to get $250.00, which is the amount of our monthly depreciation.

<u>Part 2 calculates the monthly finance charge:</u> First, we have to convert our interest rate to a money factor. We do that by dividing the interest rate (.08 for 8%) by 24, which gives us our money factor (.00333). Then we add the net cap cost ($20,000) to the residual ($11,000) to get $31,000 which we multiply by the factor (.00333). The final result ($103.23) is our monthly lease rate.

<u>Part 3 calculates the total payment:</u> Using the results of Part 1 and Part 2, we add the amount of monthly depreciation ($250.00) to the monthly lease rate ($103.23) to get $353.23, our monthly payment *without sales tax*. Sales tax on a lease is based on the monthly payment (and cap reduction), so we would add an additional $24.73 to the payment if our state had a tax rate of 7%.

With this information, we can now finish Worksheet #1.

Worksheet #2 — Lease Payment Calculation

Part 1: Monthly Depreciation
[Term is the length of the lease in months.]
Monthly Depreciation =
> (Net Cap Cost — Residual) ÷ Term

Net Cap Cost	*20,000*
Minus Residual	*11,000*
Total	*9,000*
÷ Term	*36*
Monthly Depreciation	*250.00*

Part 2: Lease Rate (Monthly Finance Charge)
Money Factor = APR [.xxx] ÷ 24
Lease Rate = (Net Cap Cost + Residual) X Money Factor

Net Cap Cost	*20,000*
Plus Residual	*11,000*
Total	*31,000*
Times Money Factor	*.00333*
Monthly Lease Rate	*103.23*

Part 3: Total Monthly Payment
Monthly Payment = Monthly Depreciation + Lease Rate
(Plus applicable sales tax on the total monthly payment)

Monthly Depreciation	*250.00*
Plus Monthly Lease Rate	*103.23*
Monthly Payment	*353.23*
(Plus Sales Tax)	
(Monthly Payment w/Tax)	

Now that we know the amount of the monthly lease payment, we can complete Worksheet #1.

We enter the monthly payment ($353.23) in the "Lease Terms" section, along with the money factor. To get the total of monthly payments, we multiply the monthly payment by 36 (the term), which gives us $12,716.28.

The security deposit is usually an amount that's equal to one month's payment rounded up to the next multiple of 25, and it may have a minimum amount that applies in cases where the monthly payment is real low. (Assume the security deposit will be at least $300.) Since the monthly payment on our lease is $353, we round that up to $375 for the amount of our security deposit.

Under "Amounts due at lease signing," we enter the $375 for our security deposit, and $353.23 for the first month's payment. Then we add up the numbers in the "Amounts due" column and enter the results ($1,578.23) for "Total due at lease signing."

For the last item, "Total cost", we add up the total cap cost reduction (which is zero), the total of monthly payments ($12,716.28), the acquisition fee ($450), and the title fees ($400), entering the result ($13,566.28) as the total cost of the lease *without sales tax*. (A sales tax rate of 7% would add $890.28 to the total.)

On the pages following this worksheet, we've added a $2,000 cap reduction to the previous lease to show how that would affect the monthly payments.

Worksheet #1 — Lease Information

Vehicle year, make, model ___*1997 LeaseMobile XLT*___
Retail price (MSRP) ___*22,000*___

Vehicle Price:

A. Negotiated vehicle price ___*20,000*___

B. Add-ons: (warranty, insurance, etc.)

_____

C. Gross cap cost (A+B) ___*20,000*___

Credits:

D. Cash down payment ___*0*___

E. Net trade-in allowance ___*0*___

F. Rebates ___*0*___

G. Total cap cost reduction (D+E+F) ___*0*___

Lease Terms:

Net cap cost (C minus G) ___*20,000*___

Term _*36*_ Money factor _*.00333*_ Interest rate _*8%*_

Monthly payment ___*353.23*___ Residual value _*11,000*_

H. Total of monthly payments ___*12,716.28*___

Amounts due at lease signing:

Cash down payment (optional) _____

Net trade-in allowance (optional) _____

Refundable security deposit ___*375*___

1) Acquisition fee ___*450*___

2) Title/registration fees ___*400*___

3) Sales tax on cap reduction (G) _____

First month's payment ___*353.23*___

Total due at lease signing ___*1,578.23*___

Total cost of lease (G+H+1+2+3) ___*13,566.28*___

In this worksheet, we've added a $2,000 cap reduction to the price and terms from the previous lease, to illustrate the dramatic effect down payments have on the monthly payments in a lease.

We fill in the worksheet with same prices as before: retail price $22,000 and negotiated price $20,000. This time, we enter $2,000 as a cash down payment under "Credits," giving us a total cap cost reduction (G) of $2,000.

Under "Lease Terms," we enter $18,000 as the net cap cost. The term is still 36 (for the number of months), the APR is still 8%, and the residual is still $11,000. *Notice that the down payment did not affect the residual (or purchase option price), which is based on MSRP.*

Under "Amounts due at lease signing," we enter $2,000 on the "cash down payment" line. The acquisition fee is still $450 and the title fees are still estimated at $400.

Notice that we listed the acquisition fee and title fees under "Amounts due at lease signing." In most cases, you would be required to pay these up front. However, in a few rare instances, you may see a lease offered with no up-front money required. If these fees are added into the cap cost and financed for several years, the total finance charges will be a lot higher. Worse yet, you will be severely "upside-down" (meaning the vehicle is worth less than the loan balance), which could result in even larger penalties in the event of early termination.

Whether you're leasing or buying, it's not smart to finance any taxes, license fees, or any other "paperwork" charges, so be sure to pay these up front. Try to avoid the "upside-down" loan-to-value situation.

Now let's go to Worksheet #2.

Worksheet #1 — Lease Information

Vehicle year, make, model ___*1997 LeaseMobile XLT*___
Retail price (MSRP) ____*22,000*____

Vehicle Price:

A. Negotiated vehicle price ____*20,000*____

B. Add-ons: (warranty, insurance, etc.)

_____

C. Gross cap cost (A+B) _____*20,000*_____

Credits:

D. Cash down payment ____*2,000*____

E. Net trade-in allowance _____*0*_____

F. Rebates _____*0*_____

G. Total cap cost reduction (D+E+F) _____*2,000*_____

Lease Terms:

Net cap cost (C minus G) _____*18,000*_____

Term _*36*_ Money factor _____ Interest rate _*8%*_

Monthly payment _____ Residual value _*11,000*_

H. Total of monthly payments _____

Amounts due at lease signing:

Cash down payment (optional) ____*2,000*____

Net trade-in allowance (optional) _____

Refundable security deposit _____

1) Acquisition fee ____*450*____

2) Title/registration fees ____*400*____

3) Sales tax on cap reduction (G) _____

First month's payment _____

Total due at lease signing _____

Total cost of lease (G+H+1+2+3) _____

In Worksheet #2, we use the net cap cost, residual, term, and interest rate from our Lease Information sheet.

<u>Part 1:</u> We subtract the residual ($11,000) from the net cap cost ($18,000), which gives us $7,000. We divide that by the term (36), getting $194.44 for our monthly depreciation.

<u>Part 2:</u> Since we're still using 8% for the interest rate, our money factor is still .00333 (.08 ÷ 24 = .00333). Now we add the net cap cost ($18,000) to the residual ($11,000), getting $29,000. When we multiply that total ($29,000) by the money factor (.00333), we get $96.57, our new monthly lease rate.

<u>Part 3:</u> Using the results of Part 1 and Part 2, we add the monthly depreciation ($194.44) to the lease rate ($96.57), getting $291.01, our new monthly payment *without sales tax.* (If our state had a sales tax rate of 7%, we would add an additional $20.37 to the monthly payment.)

Using this information, we can now finish Worksheet #1.

Note on Ford Interest Rate Quotes

You may run into the following situation when gathering information to calculate payments: If you ask a Ford dealer for the interest rate (or money factor) on a particular lease, you may discover that your calculations (using their money rates) show lower monthly finance charges than the ones quoted by the dealer. Ford Motor Credit adds a hidden administrative fee to their monthly lease rate, which makes the effective APR 1.5 to 2 points higher than the rate quoted by the dealer. This often results in real rates of 10-11% when other lenders only charge 9%.

Worksheet #2 — Lease Payment Calculation

Part 1: Monthly Depreciation
[Term is the length of the lease in months.]
Monthly Depreciation =
$$(Net\ Cap\ Cost - Residual) \div Term$$

Net Cap Cost	18,000
Minus Residual	11,000
Total	7,000
÷ Term	36
Monthly Depreciation	194.44

Part 2: Lease Rate (Monthly Finance Charge)
Money Factor = APR [.xxx] ÷ 24
Lease Rate = (Net Cap Cost + Residual) X Money Factor

Net Cap Cost	18,000
Plus Residual	11,000
Total	29,000
Times Money Factor	.00333
Monthly Lease Rate	96.57

Part 3: Total Monthly Payment
Monthly Payment = Monthly Depreciation + Lease Rate
(Plus applicable sales tax on the total monthly payment)

Monthly Depreciation	194.44
Plus Monthly Lease Rate	96.57
Monthly Payment	291.01
(Plus Sales Tax)	
(Monthly Payment w/Tax)	

Now that we know the amount of the monthly lease payment, we can complete Worksheet #1.

We enter the monthly payment ($291.01) in the "Lease Terms" section, along with the money factor. To get the total of monthly payments, we multiply $291.01 by 36 (months), which gives us $10,476.36.

Since our monthly payment is now $291.01, we round that up to $300 for the security deposit.

Under "Amounts due at lease signing," we enter the $300 for our security deposit, and $291.01 for the first month's payment. Then we add up the numbers in the "Amounts due" column and enter the results ($3,441.01) for "Total due at lease signing."

For the last item, "Total cost", we add up the total cap cost reduction ($2,000), the total of monthly payments ($10,476.36), the acquisition fee ($450), and the title fees ($400), entering the result ($13,326.36) as the total cost of the lease *without sales tax*. (A sales tax rate of 7% would add $873.32 to the total.)

Notice that the $2,000 down reduced our monthly payment from $353 to $291. (On a similar 24-month lease, the payment would have dropped about $90.) Any combination of rebates, cash, or trade-in credit totaling $2,000 would have the same effect as that amount in cash.

Even though we put $2,000 down, the total cost of the lease only dropped by $240. All we really "saved" was $240 in finance charges—because we borrowed less money.

Worksheet #1 — Lease Information

Vehicle year, make, model ___*1997 LeaseMobile XLT*___

Retail price (MSRP) _____*22,000*_____

Vehicle Price:

A. Negotiated vehicle price _____*20,000*_____

B. Add-ons: (warranty, insurance, etc.)

_____

C. <u>Gross cap cost</u> (A+B) _____*20,000*_____

Credits:

D. Cash down payment _____*2,000*_____

E. Net trade-in allowance _____*0*_____

F. Rebates _____*0*_____

G. <u>Total cap cost reduction</u> (D+E+F) _____*2,000*_____

Lease Terms:

<u>Net cap cost</u> (C minus G) _____*18,000*_____

Term _*36*_ Money factor _*.00333*_ Interest rate _*8%*_

Monthly payment _*291.01*_ Residual value _*11,000*_

H. <u>Total of monthly payments</u> _____*10,476.36*_____

Amounts due at lease signing:

Cash down payment (optional) _____*2,000*_____

Net trade-in allowance (optional) _____

Refundable security deposit _____*300*_____

1) Acquisition fee _____*450*_____

2) Title/registration fees _____*400*_____

3) Sales tax on cap reduction (G) _____

First month's payment _____*291.01*_____

<u>Total due at lease signing</u> _____*3,441.01*_____

Total cost of lease (G+H+1+2+3) _____*13,326.36*_____

Leasing Lessons for Smart Shoppers

5

Comparing Costs:
Leasing vs. Buying

Beware of salespeople who compare lease payments with
3-year or 4-year payments on a conventional loan. Why?
Because comparing payments on similar terms is mean-
ingless and often deceptive: Leasing is simply long-term
"renting" of a vehicle—there's no equity or ownership, so
the payments are supposed to be a lot lower.

And watch out for salespeople quoting "packed payments" for loans and leases. For example, Laura the
Lease Manager told me that a 48-month loan on $18,000
would cost me $514 per month, but a 2-year lease pay-
ment on the same car would only be $472. Both deals in-

volved a $4,500 down payment, and both were inflated—
at the current APR offered by other lenders, the loan payment should have been only $439. (See Table 2. On a 5-
year loan, the payment would have only been $365 per
month, making her lease look even worse. *I guess she
just forgot to mention that.*) And the lease payment she
quoted was about $172 too high: she was trying to use the
"disappearing down payment" trick, too.

This "packed payment" trick serves two purposes:
First, if only the loan payment is inflated, it makes the
lease look like a better deal than it really is. And second,
by inflating both lease and loan payments in a deceptive
comparison, it makes it easier to get away with some kind
of hidden overcharge in the lease. *This is why you should
always figure out your own loan and lease payments.*

The following sections offer examples and information on comparisons of leasing versus buying. Also,
worksheets are provided at the end of the book (in the
Appendix) to make it easy for you to compare costs.

Short-Term Leasing vs. Short-Term Buying

When looked at long-term, leasing costs more than buying. However, when comparing two short-term periods,
leasing may not look too bad (because the huge depreciation expense of the first two years makes both expensive).
And in some cases, mostly those with large manufacturer
subsidies, leasing might even be cheaper. Here's how to
do a short-term comparison using a "typical" price, residual, interest rate, and wholesale value:

We'll compare lease and loan payments on a $20,000
car, no down payment, both at 8% APR. The terms will
be 3 years on the lease and 5 years on the loan, with the
loan terminated—and the car sold—at the end of 3 years.
(Why use a 5-year term on the loan? Because that's the

term that most people choose when they're buying. Plus, on a 3-year lease, you'll pay almost as much interest as you would on a 5-year loan, so the two are very similar in total costs.)

In our example, monthly lease payments would be $378 and loan payments would be $406 (from Tables 1-2 in the Appendix), a difference of only $28. On the loan, you would owe $8,966 at the end of 3 years, and the car would be worth at least $10,000 to $11,000 wholesale—more if you sold it yourself.

The extra $28 per month that the loan costs over the lease adds up to $1,008 over 3 years, which would cancel out most (or all) of the profit if you sold the car at the end of 3 years. (If you got more than $10,000 for the car, the purchase would come out ahead of the lease, otherwise it's about even.) Factor in lease expenses of $450-800 for acquisition/disposition fees, and the scales might tip in favor of the conventional purchase.

How can you get a short-term lease that's cheaper than a purchase? Find one with a subsidized residual and interest rate: Looking at Table 8, notice that a four-point residual increase saves $20 per month on the 3-year lease example, and Table 3 shows a savings of $25 per month from a two-point APR discount. The combined savings from those subsidies would be $1,620 over 3 years, making the lease a lot more attractive.

Short-Term Leasing vs. Long-Term Buying

No matter what a salesman tells you, the total cost of a long-term purchase will always be a lot lower than the cost of multiple short-term leases. The reason: depreciation. Most new cars lose about 40% of their value in the first two years, so if you get three 2-year leases in a row, you'll be paying for 120% of a car—plus interest—and you'll have nothing but cancelled checks at the end of the third lease.

Since most people keep their cars for at least 6 years (7.8 to be exact), we'll use that term of ownership in a comparison with two consecutive 3-year leases on the same car. The terms are the same as before: $20,000 car, 3-year lease and 5-year loan, 8% APR for both. Here's how the comparison works:

On the purchase side, you would make 60 payments of $406 which totals $24,360. At the end of 6 years, you would own a car that's worth around $5,000 to $6,000. If you sold it for $5,000 at that point, your net cost of ownership would only be $19,360 for 6 years.

On the 3-year lease, you would be paying $378 for 36 months, which totals $13,608. Since you need a car for another 3 years, you lease again at the same terms, spending another $13,608. At the end of 6 years, you've spent $27,216 to "rent" two cars (and maybe another $900 in acquisition fees).

Now, the "leasing specialists" would argue that you would have to pay a lot of repair bills if you kept that car for 3 more years. (Are they implying that their cars aren't built very well? If that's a valid point, maybe you should find a better car—at another dealer.) Nice try, guys, but the increased insurance and registration costs from leasing a new car every two or three years will usually cancel out any "savings" from not having to pay for repairs.

As you can see from our example, it's about $8,000 cheaper to buy a car and keep it than it is to continue leasing. But it won't have that "new car smell," and only you can decide how much that's worth.

6

What's a Good Lease Deal?
(And How to Get One)

Out of all those advertised lease deals, how can you tell which ones are actually bargains? Aren't all leases good deals because they have "low" monthly payments? *No, but that's exactly what the advertisers want you to think.*

All lease deals with low monthly payments are not alike: many require large down payments or trade equity, and almost all have real low mileage limits. Don't fall for the often-used "down payment trick" — that $300 a month with $2,400 down is a better deal than $400 a month with zero down (for 24 months). The "real cost" is the same on both. (Remember: down payments are simply monthly payments paid up-front, they don't reduce the residual or purchase option price.)

A lot of advertised low-payment leases are nothing but "bait-and-switch" tricks. They usually apply to one vehicle only (which will be "sold" just before you get there, of course), or they're for "stripped" models that will cost a lot more after adding air conditioning or other popular options. And the most common "bargain" leases are on cars that are selling poorly (i.e., no one wants them).

If you're lucky enough to find a zero-down, low-payment lease on a car that's equipped exactly the way you want, with a high enough mileage limit for your driving habits, then you won't have much homework to do. Just make sure it really is a low payment, not just one that seems low because of a dishonest comparison by a salesman. (By "zero down," I mean no cap reduction. You'll still have to pay the first month's payment and security deposit, and maybe an acquisition fee, up-front.)

The best way to make sure that a lease deal is, in fact, a "bargain" is to know exactly what the monthly payment should be, based on zero down, using the best available rates on car loans at banks and credit unions, and using the current residual estimate from the *Automotive Lease Guide*. And don't forget to include a large discount off the retail price, since that will cause a dramatic reduction in the monthly payment.

Chapter 4 explains how to calculate payments, and there are worksheets and tables in the Appendix that will make it fairly easy to do this yourself. That's the only way to be sure that you're getting a good deal. Thousands of leasing victims made the mistake of trusting a salesman who told them what a good deal they were getting.

The following sections will explain what information you need, where to get it, and what to do with it, all aimed at helping you to get a great lease deal. And two great shortcuts are included that could save you a lot of time and money.

Chapter 8: Resources for Getting the Best Deal

Complete information on all of the reference material and services mentioned in the following sections can be found in Chapter 8, "The Homework Section." Addresses, prices, and phone numbers are provided for resources that must be ordered by mail or phone.

What Is a Good Lease Deal?

By now, you should have read Chapter 5, "Comparing Costs: Leasing vs. Buying," so you'll understand how to do an honest comparison of the two. If you haven't, the following information may not make sense, so go back and read it before proceeding with this section.

A good lease deal has a monthly payment that's a lot lower than a 5-year loan payment on a purchase, using the same down payment and interest rate. If the difference is only about $40 or less, the lease is definitely not a bargain, and it will cost more (long-term) than buying. Try to get a lease payment that's at least $70-80 less than a 5-year loan payment; $100 less would be a real bargain.

For example, on a $15,000 car, the monthly payments to buy it are $304 per month with no down payment, an APR of 8% and a 5-year term. (See Tables 1 and 2 in the Appendix.) Unsubsidized lease payments on the same car (3-year term, same APR, and zero down) would be $283. That's not a good deal, because you're only saving $21 per month with no ownership. A good deal on that car would be closer to $200 per month with zero down.

Since a lease is really just a long-term rental with no

real ownership or equity, you should focus on getting the smallest down payment combined with the lowest monthly payment. Whenever possible, always use "zero down" for figuring payments. If you're going to make a down payment, just make sure you're getting proper credit and a significant reduction in the monthly payment.

To see the proper effect that down payments have on monthly payments, see Tables 5-7 in the Appendix. *The effect of $1,000 down is the same as a $1,000 price reduction.* Looking at Table 5, notice that the 2-year lease payment on a $20,000 car is $439, but it's only $394 with a $1,000 price reduction—or $1,000 down. (And that price cut is easy to get on a car in this price range.)

Using Table 5 again, notice what *should* happen if you got a $1,000 price reduction *and* made a down payment of $1,000 on that same car, at the same term: the monthly payment should drop from $439 to $349. Many people have been cheated because they didn't know this and dealers gave them a smaller discount, or they just inflated the cap cost to steal the down payment without any reduction in the monthly payment at all.

Table 3 shows the effect of APR changes on monthly payments: On a 2-year lease, a secret APR boost of two points will raise your monthly payment by $26. *Now you can see why you should figure out your own payments.* If you don't, it will be a lot easier to take advantage of you.

To get a great lease deal, you need to negotiate the cap cost down as low as possible—around dealer invoice on most cars, lower if the dealer is getting additional incentives. And you need to get the lowest possible APR and the highest possible residual (see Table 8). The only way to do that is to find a vehicle that has a factory-subsidized residual and/or interest rate. You may see these advertised, but you can always call the automakers or dealers to find out which models have them. If a lease doesn't meet these criteria, it will cost you more (long-term) than a conventional purchase, so it wouldn't be considered a good deal.

Warning: If you decide to take advantage of one of these "bargain" leases, whatever you do, don't buy the car at the end of the lease unless you negotiate a dramatically reduced price from the residual amount.

The Truth About "Dealer Cost"

To get the best possible lease deal, you have to find out the dealer's real cost so you'll know how low they can go on a car. Most people think that "dealer invoice" is the actual dealer cost on a new car, but in most cases it isn't. Dealers often get factory-to-dealer incentives that reduce their cost below invoice, and smart shoppers who know this buy and lease cars at (or below) dealer invoice all the time.

Getting the "Magic Numbers"

Here are the "magic numbers" you'll need to be sure that you're getting the best possible deal: the dealer invoice, dealer holdback, any dealer and/or customer incentives, the residual from the current *Automotive Lease Guide,* and the MSRP. (You'll also need the residual and APR that the dealer is using, which you can get from the dealer.)

The best source for accurate, current information is Fighting Chance of Long Beach, California. They can tell you the real dealer cost—including secret incentives, as well as other useful information that will help you get a good deal. And they can also provide the latest residual numbers from the *Automotive Lease Guide*. They really do give consumers a "Fighting Chance" in the new-car game. (See Chapter 8.)

The Best Time to Lease

The best time to lease is at the very beginning of the model year, when the residual is at its highest level. After a new model comes out, the residual will usually drop one or two percentage points every two months, which means your monthly payments will be higher if the leasing company doesn't provide a residual or APR subsidy.

If you're tempted to lease last year's model after the new ones are out, make sure it's got a big subsidy on the residual, or your monthly payments may be as high as those on a newer model. (Be sure to check the current *Automotive Lease Guide* to see if a residual is inflated or not.) This is also true of the current year model that's been out for 6 months or more: if it's not heavily subsidized, you should pass. Wait until the new ones come out and you may find a lower payment on a newer car.

The best time to "deal" is usually towards the end of the month, or towards the end of a volume-based dealer incentive program. This is where the dealer gets extra cash for reaching a sales goal for a specific model, and it can really motivate them to sell a car on a low-profit deal. (This information is part of the Fighting Chance package. See Chapter 8.)

SHORTCUT #1: CarBargains & *LeaseWise*

The easiest way to get a good deal is to use CarBargains or their new service, *LeaseWise*. CarBargains will get you at least five competing bids on a purchase, which you can then use to negotiate a lease deal. Or you can just use *LeaseWise* to get at least five competing bids on the lowest-cost lease. (See Chapter 7.)

SHORTCUT #2: The Fax (or Mail) Strategy

The strategy involves getting a number of dealers to make blind bids on a new car, without you being there. This has two big advantages: 1) they know that you will lease somewhere else if their bid isn't the lowest, and 2) since you're not there, they can't use any of their tricks to get more money out of you.

Make a list of all the dealers you would be willing to lease from, then call them on the phone to get the names of their fleet managers along with their mailing addresses (or fax numbers). If a dealer doesn't have a fleet manager, get the name of the sales manager instead.

Draft a convincing letter to be sent to all the fleet managers on your list. The letters should be identical with the exception of the manager/dealer identification, and they must communicate that you are a serious and knowledgeable customer.

In the letter, state that you are going to lease a specific model new vehicle, listing the color and any options, then ask them to quote you their best price for a specific term. (Stick to 30-36 months; 2 years is too expensive and any longer than 3 years is not a good idea.) Mention that you are also getting quotes from other dealers in your area and the one with the lowest quote gets your business. Let them know you're aware of the dealer invoice and any factory-to-dealer incentives, so you expect the most competitive bids to be at (or below) MSRP. Remind them to leave the customer rebate money (if applicable) out of their quotes; that money belongs to the buyer, so don't let the dealers use it to make their bids look better than they really are. (In special factory-subsidized lease deals, the rebate/incentive may not be available.)

Be sure to mention that you do not want anything added to the car that's not factory-installed, especially paint sealer, fabric protection, undercoating, alarm system, etc. Ask them to quote the cap cost, APR, residual, monthly payment, and any additional charges.

Your letter should have your name and address, both home and work phone numbers, and a fax number if you have one. Close with the statement that you will be making a final decision in two weeks, so you will assume that dealers who fail to respond by then are not interested. Thank them in advance, sign your name, and fax or mail the letters. Then wait for a response.

Some dealers won't respond to this approach because they would rather have the "home court advantage," so be sure to send out at least five or six letters. If any of the managers try to get you to come in before quoting a firm price, tell them you're not interested in doing business that way.

If you're doing this by fax, follow up a week later with phone calls to the dealers who didn't respond. Ask if they received your letter and whether they would like to provide a quote. (They'll usually let you know right away whether they're interested—or mad that you're too smart to fall for any of their sales tricks.)

By the time the quotes start coming in, you should already know what a good deal would look like, because you read this book and used the worksheets to calculate your own payments. If the best lease deal has a cap cost that's at or below invoice with an inflated residual (a low APR would be nice, too), and the math on the payment calculations checks out—take it.

The Hard Way: Negotiating in Person

It's harder to negotiate a minimum-profit deal in person, because you'll probably have to deal with a salesman who gets paid a percentage of the gross profit on each deal.

So before talking to any salesmen, try to get an appointment with the fleet or sales manager. If you can deal directly with them, any transaction will be considered a "house sale" with no sales commission.

Make a list of all the dealers in your area who sell the line of cars you're interested in. Your "showroom strategy" will be to visit the first dealer on your list and make one low (but tempting) offer, letting them know that you plan on making the same offer at their competitors if they reject it.

If a dealer rejects your offer, ask if they would like to make a written counteroffer that you might consider after you've visited the other dealers. Then get up, politely thank them for their time, ask for their business card, and leave. *Don't increase your offer on the first visit.*

If you're dealing with a salesman, there are two things you should know: First, no matter what he says about your offer being too low, insist that it be written up and presented to management. Tell him to communicate the fact that that is your only offer and insist that he get a written response from his manager. Then tell him that you can only wait ten minutes for an answer because you have other appointments to keep. (That way he can't keep you there all day to stop you from visiting competing dealers. Why would he do that? Because he's afraid that one of them will accept your offer.)

The second thing you should know is that after your offer is rejected, salesmen will almost always follow you to your car and try all kinds of tricks to get you back inside, but don't fall for them. Just ask if they decided to accept your offer, and if the answer isn't a firm "yes," then leave. In most cases, the dealer will give in if you made them a decent offer—but only after you walk out. *Your best negotiating weapon is your ability (and willingness) to walk out after a dealer rejects your offer.*

If your initial offer contains just enough profit to tempt some of the dealers, you probably won't have to visit that many before someone agrees to your price. And if they all reject your offer, raise it $200 and start over. Don't pay more than 2% over invoice; if you can't do better than that, you should call CarBargains.

How much profit should be tempting? That depends on the price range: $400-500 profit should be tempting on a car that sells for $12,000 to $14,000. You'll probably have to offer $600-700 profit on a $20,000 car, and maybe $1,000 or more on a luxury car. And when you're determining dealer's cost, always include holdback and any dealer incentives, which means that you might be able to get a price that's below invoice.

If you have an old car you might want to trade in, don't discuss it until after you have negotiated a good price on the new car. You'll always get more money selling the old car yourself, because a dealer is never going to pay more than wholesale for it. But if you don't want to be bothered with the sale of a used car, take it to the used car departments at several dealers and ask them to make an offer.

To be a successful negotiator, you need to be seen as a serious, well-informed, unemotional buyer who has no preference for one dealer over another. And don't let on that you're in love with a particular car. Repeat this over and over, until you really believe it: *It's just a car.* Say it in front of the dealer or salesman, too, because they hate to hear it. They want to convince you that a car is "an investment," but if it is, it's probably the worst investment you'll ever make, so try to make it a less expensive one. Say it again: *It's just a car.* Now, go out and get a great deal!

7

CarBargains & *LeaseWise:*
Shortcuts to Savings

Some people just don't have the ability (or the desire) to do battle with car dealers, so arming them with industry secrets is not going to save them any money when they lease (or buy) a new car. So, should these people just resign themselves to paying hundreds or thousands more than someone else for the same car or truck? Absolutely not—they should use CarBargains or *LeaseWise!*

CarBargains is a service provided by the Center for the Study of Services, a non-profit consumer group in Washington, D.C. Unlike auto brokers and other car buying services that are "for-profit" and may be affiliated with specific dealers, CarBargains is completely independent and does not take any money from dealers for steering buyers toward a particular dealer. CarBargains shops many different dealers to get its customers the best prices on new vehicles and is the only service that I recommend.

To see how CarBargains measured up to several other large car buying services, *Kiplinger's Personal Finance Magazine* conducted a test for their December, 1992 publication. *Kiplinger's* used four services, including CarBargains, to shop for three popular cars: a Lexus LS 400 (retail $47,000), a Ford Taurus GL sedan (retail $18,393), and a Geo Prizm sedan (retail $11,907). At that time, many Lexus dealers were so confident they could sell their cars without cutting prices that they refused to deal with buying services. Only CarBargains was able to quote a lower price on the Lexus.

CarBargains
—Lexus: $5,704 below retail
—Taurus: $2,519 below retail
—Geo: $681 below retail

Amway Motoring Plan (members only)
—Lexus: no quote
—Taurus: $2,244 below retail
—Geo: $496 below retail

CarPuter (limited to approx. 500 dealers)
—Lexus: no quote
—Taurus: $2,298 below retail
—Geo: $598 below retail

Nationwide Auto Brokers
—Lexus: no quote
—Taurus: $2,212 below retail
—Geo: $561 below retail

As you can see, CarBargains was clearly the winner in the *Kiplinger's* test, resulting in dealer bids that were

$83 to $185 lower than the other services on the Geo, $221 to $307 lower on the Taurus, and $5,704 lower on the Lexus.

In another test of car buying services done in 1992 by *The Washingtonian Magazine*, CarBargains got lower dealer bids than Price Club and the United Buying Service. The results of their test, shopping for a new Honda Civic sedan, are as follows:

CarBargains	$11,575
Price Club	$12,940
United Buying Service	$12,782

How CarBargains Works

CarBargains will make dealers compete with each other for your business, allowing you to avoid the unpleasant (and often costly) experience of negotiating on a new vehicle. They are so confident of their ability to get you the best possible deal that their service has a money-back guarantee: *If you are able to buy a car at a price lower then the best quote included in their report without using their information, they will gladly refund your entire fee.*

To use CarBargains, call toll-free (800) 475-7283. The fee for their service is $150 which can be paid by check or credit card. If you decide to order by mail, make your check payable to "CarBargains" and specify the year, make, and model of the vehicle you wish to buy. Include a daytime phone number and mail your request to:

CarBargains
733 15th Street NW, Suite 820
Washington, DC 20005

The following is a brief description of how the Car-Bargains service works:

1. You tell them the year, make, model, and style of the car or truck you wish to buy (for example, "1996 Ford Taurus LX 4-Door Sedan").

2. Within two weeks, CarBargains will get at least five dealers in your area to bid against each other on the vehicle you requested. Each dealer will commit to a specific dollar amount above (or below) the "factory invoice" price of the vehicle.

3. You will receive a report that includes:

   • Dealer quote sheets showing how much above (or below) factory invoice cost each dealer has agreed to sell, and listing the names of the sales managers at each dealer responsible for the commitment.

   • Factory invoice cost information for your type of car or truck, showing what all dealers pay for the base vehicle and for each possible option.

   • Other useful information: on the value of your used car (based on a description you have given them), low-cost financing options, pros and cons of extended warranties/service contracts, how you may be able to get a service contract as good as your dealer offers at a substantially lower cost, etc.

4. You visit one or more of the dealers and...

   • Look at the vehicles on the lot;
   • Select the specific vehicle you want;

- Use the information they've sent you to determine the factory invoice cost of the vehicle you've selected;
- See the sales manager listed on your report's dealer quote sheets and purchase the vehicle at the factory invoice cost plus (or minus) the amount agreed to by the dealer.
- If a vehicle with the options you want is not available on a dealer's lot, you can have the dealer order the vehicle (if available) from the factory, or from another dealer, at the agreed markup (or markdown) figure.

COMMON QUESTIONS
on CarBargains

Can't I do this myself?

Dealers know that CarBargains' bidding is for real — they know they will actually get at least 5 quotes. In addition, they know that a consumer who has paid for the CarBargains service is almost certain to buy immediately from one of the quoting dealers, so refusing to quote means losing a sale. However, when you call for a bid, the dealer may not believe that you will bother to get bids elsewhere. Worse yet, dealers often refuse to bid over the phone with consumers, using lines such as, "shop around, then come on down — we'll beat anyone else's price." They don't usually take "telephone shoppers" seriously.

Dealers know that CarBargains will get bids from other dealers, so each dealership knows it will have to bid real low to have any chance of winning. They remind dealers of any ongoing factory-to-dealer incentive programs, manufacturer holdbacks, carryover allowances, and other factors that give the dealer room to cut his price. Also, dealers know that if CarBargains doesn't get good prices locally, they will get quotes from dealers outside the area who will deliver locally.

CarBargains is a witness to the dealers' quotes; they get signed commitments by fax and dealers know they will follow up. On the other hand, if a customer gets a quote by phone, some dealers may feel they can back out without serious consequences.

The CarBargains staff are car-buying experts. They make sure all costs (advertising association fees, processing fees, dealer-installed options, etc.) are included in the dealers' bids, not added on later.

How close will the dealers be to my home?

CarBargains has a computer file of all dealers in the country. When you order their service, they identify dealers close to you and get them to bid. You can even have them include (or leave out) a dealer of your choice.

Will I still get a factory rebate?

Your CarBargains report will tell you whether the car you are buying has a factory-to-customer rebate. If it does, you can choose to keep the rebate money, or you can use it for part (or all) of the down payment.

Do I have to decide which options I want before calling CarBargains?

No. You only need to tell them the year, make, model, and style of car you want. The dealers bid a specific dollar amount above (or below) the factory invoice price. CarBargains will send you a printout that lists the factory invoice prices for the base vehicle and for each available factory-installed option. This allows you to decide which options you want later, while still being able to figure out the total factory invoice amount.

Is CarBargains able to get any car at a discount price?

Almost—the only car that's *never* available at a discount is a Saturn. Certain models that are in short supply may sell at a premium for a brief period (like the first Mazda Miatas), but most cars and trucks are available somewhere at a dealer who's willing to sell at a substantial discount.

How much can CarBargains save me on popular models?

Results will vary depending on the time of year, whether any factory-to-dealer incentives are in effect, and from one region to another. Each year there is relatively little discounting of new model-year vehicles in the first few months after introduction, but CarBargains consistently gets great prices for their customers. Examples cited by CarBargains include:

1997 Acura RL 4Dr Sdn	Dealer invoice
1997 Buick LeSabre 4Dr	$450 below invoice
1997 Chrysler Sebring 2Dr	$100 below invoice
1997 Ford Explorer 4Dr	Dealer invoice
1997 Ford Windstar GL	$100 below invoice
1997 Honda Accord 4Dr	Dealer invoice
1997 Isuzu Rodeo 4Dr	$1,400 below invoice
1997 Lexus LS400	$1,000 below invoice
1997 Subaru Legacy 4Dr	$550 below invoice
1997 Toyota Camry 4Dr	Invoice + $200

However, some models are never sold below invoice. Sometimes the best available price may, in fact, be the full "window sticker" price, which could be 5% to 23% above dealer invoice, depending on the model.

As is the case with many other products, car prices are usually determined by supply and demand (and negotiating ability). For consumers, the goal should be to find the best price that is available when they are ready to buy. The CarBargains service is designed to find that price by making car dealers bid for the consumer's business. It not only produces a good price, it also spares the consumer the hassles and high-pressure sales tactics often associated with buying a new car.

Consumers can use the CarBargains service to find a good "purchase" price, which they can then use as the cap cost to negotiate their own lease deal.

LeaseWise

LeaseWise is a new service offered by CarBargains that provides competitive bidding among dealers to get the lowest-cost leases. The cost is $290 and includes purchase price and lease payment bids from at least five dealers. Information is also provided on the following: residuals, interest rates, money factors, excess mileage charges, other related fees, and total cost.

LeaseWise stands alone as the first (and only) service to provide competitive bidding on leases. Four stars!!

8

The Homework Section: Resources for Getting the Best Deal

An impulsive or emotional shopper always ends up with the worst deal (or a bad case of "buyer's remorse") so avoid that mistake by taking the time to become a cool, calm, educated buyer. Promise yourself that the purpose of your first dealer visits will be *to look at everything and buy nothing*. Don't bring your checkbook or the title to your car, and don't agree to buy (or lease) anything—no matter how good it looks or sounds.

When you are visiting dealerships, salesmen will swarm around you even though you tell them you're "just looking." Tell them you're not going to buy anything for three or four weeks and they'll usually disappear, allowing you to take your time looking at different models. Collect brochures and other information, and don't be afraid to ask questions. Then go home—in your old car.

After visiting dealers to see which cars you like (and can afford), the next step is to research those models to see what kind of ratings they have, and also to see if they have any "twins or cousins" that may be less expensive. Even though you probably won't be interested in keeping the vehicle after the lease ends (otherwise you would be buying, not leasing), you should still research its track record for safety, repairs, fuel economy, insurance cost, and future resale value. Whether you're leasing or buying, any one of these items has the potential to ruin your new car experience.

After a brief explanation of these important features (and a few other things you should know), you'll find a resource section containing the best sources I've found for the information you need.

Safety

Safety is always ranked by consumers as an important feature on a new car, but all cars don't offer the same crash protection, so how can shoppers tell which ones are safer? Of course, you could ask the salespeople, but do you really think they'll tell you that a competitor's cars have better safety ratings? (Probably not.) Fortunately, there are a number of organizations and publications that provide safety ratings for all the new cars every year.

Repair History

Be sure to include a vehicle's repair history on your list of things to consider. There are significant differences in quality from one car to the next, so don't assume that your car is going to be trouble-free just because it's new. Even though you're leasing, you'll still have to pay for maintenance and repairs to keep the vehicle in good condition. If you don't, you'll be hit with a hefty penalty when you turn the vehicle in.

Checking the repair history becomes even more important if you're considering a used car lease. Before a three-year-old vehicle ends up on a used car lot, its original factory warranty will usually have expired. And the warranty on a two-year-old car might only be good for another six months (or less) if the previous owner drove at least 15,000 miles per year. Since most used cars are sold or leased without any kind of warranty, choosing the wrong car can turn out to be an expensive mistake.

Fuel Economy

Unfortunately, the cars with the best fuel economy ratings are usually the smallest and lightest models, which means they won't do very well in an accident with a larger car. (Sorry, that's physics.) Also, the most miserly vehicles are usually the ones with the smallest engines and the fewest luxury features (like air conditioning). For most people, some fuel economy will be sacrificed to gain more safety, horsepower, and/or accessories.

Insurance Cost

This item is frequently overlooked until after the new car is driven home. Of course, by that time it's too late to pick another car because the insurance is going to cost too much. Rates can vary dramatically from one model to another, so be sure to call your agent for a quote *before* you make the final decision. And don't assume you'll automatically be covered when you get a new car—let your agent know in advance when you plan on taking delivery.

A warning for new lease customers: Leases usually require higher liability coverage ($300,000) than you may normally carry, so be sure to find out what the insurance costs are going to be before signing a lease contract. And since you'll be getting a new vehicle every two or three years, your insurance payments will always be high. In states that have high insurance rates, this requirement can significantly increase the cost of driving a new car.

Depreciation (Future Resale Value)

Depreciation should be an important consideration when deciding which car to lease. Some models can lose over 60% of their value (starting from MSRP) in the first 36 months, while others may only lose 40%. Since depreciation is usually the largest part of a monthly lease payment, choosing a model with good resale value should make it easier to negotiate lower payments.

Some vehicles have poor resale value because they have a history of spending too much time in the repair shop, so keep this in mind if you're tempted to lease one anyway. Even on a three-year lease, you could easily run out of warranty before the lease is up (by driving over 12,000 miles per year), leaving you with repair bills on a car you don't own. To avoid this, check the repair history before signing any contracts.

"Twins & Cousins"

"Twins and cousins" are similar vehicles that are sold under different names. These cars usually have the same basic body style, engine, and drivetrain. In many cases, the only differences are in trim (style), levels of luxury, and/or which features are standard equipment. However, there can be significant differences in price, so you may be able to save money by purchasing the less expensive twin. (Example: Toyota Corolla and Geo Prizm)

Dealer Cost

To get the best lease deal, you have to know the dealer's real cost on a vehicle so you can figure out how much the monthly payments should be. And the "factory invoice" or "dealer invoice" figure doesn't tell the whole story—you also need up-to-date information on any factory-to-dealer incentives, allowances, and holdback money. (Be sure to read Chapter 6, "What's a Good Lease Deal?" for more on dealer's cost and how to negotiate.)

Using a Car Buying Service

For those who hate the whole negotiating process—and would normally settle for little-or-no discount off the sticker price—I recommend using a new car buying service. Instead of buying, you lease the vehicle using the discounted price as the cap cost. (See Chapter 7 for more information.)

RESOURCES

Published Ratings

Consumer Reports, Annual Auto Issue (April)
****Most comprehensive data on repair histories
****Excellent used car reliability reports
    Also—new car facts, safety & reliability ratings,
        depreciation information

The Car Book, by Jack Gillis
****Most comprehensive safety data & ratings
  Other ratings: fuel economy, maintenance costs,
    warranties, tires
  New car facts, EPA mileage figures & much more

Kiplinger's New Car Buyer's Guide
****Excellent data on resale values & insurance costs
  Plus data on mileage, interior/cargo space, and more

Books: Retail & Dealer Invoice Prices

1) *Edmund's New Car Prices*
2) *Pace Buyer's Guides, New Car Prices*
(Available in most bookstores)

Books: Used Car Prices

1) *Edmund's Used Car Prices*
2) *Kelley Blue Book/Used Car Guide, Consumer Edition*
(Available in most bookstores)

Dealer Cost & Incentive Information

FIGHTING CHANCE
5318 East 2nd Street, #242
Long Beach, CA 90803
(800) 288-1134
(310) 433-8489

**** Four stars!
Fighting Chance is the best information service I've
found. They give you the retail, invoice, and holdback
figures on the model (and options) of your choice and a
CarDeals report on dealer and customer incentives for all

vehicles so you'll know which models are being secretly discounted. They also help their customers figure lease payments, and they'll tell you how much (or how little) other informed buyers have recently paid for your chosen vehicle.

Their package also includes information on market conditions, vehicle inventories, and various negotiating strategies to help you get the best possible deal. One price covers the current and previous year model. Cost: First car $21.95 (plus $3 s&h), $8 each additional car.

Leasing Guides/Software

CHART Software
P.O. Box 145
Gilman, IL 60938
(800) 418-8450
(815) 265-7831

CHART distributes 2 leasing products:
1) *Automotive Lease Guide* contains residual and retail values that are used in determining lease payments for new and used cars. Cost: $12.50
2) "Expert Lease Pro" software will calculate lease payments, perform lease vs. buy analysis, determine the (undisclosed) cap cost or APR of a lease, figure out the dealer's profit margin, and analyze single-payment leases.
You can also print out a table of monthly payments vs. cap costs to take with you when you go to the dealer. (Or take your laptop computer to analyze their leasing deals in front of the salesman!)

One price includes software, manual, retail and invoice prices for all new cars & trucks, *Automotive Lease Guide* residual values for all new vehicles, and the latest *CarDeals* report on all customer and dealer incentives.

Cost: $69.95 for Windows or DOS version. (It will also run on a Macintosh with Softwindows.)

This is a great program! I use it to analyze leases and so do some attorneys general who are investigating fraud in the leasing business. Expert Lease has been featured in *Money Magazine, Smart Money, Kiplinger's Personal Finance Magazine,* and *Home PC.*

Car Buying & Leasing Services

CarBargains & *LeaseWise*
733 15th Street NW, Suite 820
Washington, DC 20005
(800) 475-7283
(202) 347-9612

**** Four stars!
CarBargains is the best new car buying service I've seen. (Cost: $150) They promise to get you a lower price than you can get on your own, or your money back. You can use their "purchase" bids to get your own lease, or use the *LeaseWise* service to do everything for you. (Cost: $290)

CarBargains can also provide buyers with names of dealers promising to sell factory-sponsored service contracts (extended warranties) for $50 over cost. See Chapter 7 for more information.

"Twins & Cousins"

GENERAL MOTORS:
Buick Century/Oldsmobile Cutlass
Buick LeSabre/Oldsmobile Eighty-Eight/
        Oldsmobile LSS/Pontiac Bonneville
Buick Park Avenue/Oldsmobile Ninety-Eight

Buick Regal/Oldsmobile Cutlass Supreme/
 Pontiac Grand Prix
Buick Riviera/Oldsmobile Aurora
Buick Skylark/Oldsmobile Achieva/Pontiac Grand Am
Buick Roadmaster/Chevrolet Caprice/
 Chevrolet Impala SS*
Chevrolet Astro/GMC Safari
Chevrolet Blazer/GMC Jimmy/Oldsmobile Bravada
Chevrolet Camaro/Pontiac Firebird
Chevrolet Cavalier/Pontiac Sunfire
Chevrolet Corsica/Beretta
Chevrolet Lumina/Monte Carlo
Chevrolet Lumina Minivan/Oldsmobile Silhouette/
 Pontiac Trans Sport
Chevrolet S-10 Pickup/GMC Sonoma/Isuzu Hombre
Chevrolet Suburban/GMC Suburban
Chevrolet Tahoe/GMC Yukon
*All three discontinued after 1996

FORD MOTOR COMPANY:
Ford Contour/Mercury Mystique
Ford Crown Victoria/Mercury Grand Marquis
Ford Escort/Mercury Tracer
Ford Explorer/Mercury Mountaineer
Ford Probe/Mazda 626/Mazda MX-6
Ford Ranger/Mazda B-Series Pickup
Ford Taurus/Mercury Sable
Ford Thunderbird/Mercury Cougar
Mercury Villager/Nissan Quest

CHRYSLER CORPORATION:
Chrysler Cirrus/Dodge Stratus/Plymouth Breeze
Chrysler Concorde/Dodge Intrepid/Eagle Vision
Chrysler LHS/Chrysler New Yorker
Chrysler Sebring/Dodge Avenger/Mitsubishi Galant

Chrysler Town & Country/Dodge Caravan/
Plymouth Voyager
Dodge Neon/Plymouth Neon
Dodge Stealth/Mitsubishi 3000 GT
Eagle Summit/Mitsubishi Mirage
Eagle Talon/Mitsubishi Eclipse

IMPORTS:
Acura SLX/Isuzu Trooper
Geo Metro/Suzuki Swift
Geo Prizm/Toyota Corolla
Geo Tracker/Suzuki Sidekick
Honda Odyssey/Isuzu Oasis
Honda Passport/Isuzu Rodeo
Nissan Maxima/Infiniti I30
Toyota Camry V6 XLE/Lexus ES 300
Toyota Land Cruiser/Lexus LX450

Reality Checklist for Vehicle Leasing

The National Association of Attorneys General, in cooperation with consumer advocates, has developed the Consumer Task Force Reality Checklist for Vehicle Leasing. Before signing a lease contract, have the dealer fill in the blanks on the checklist. This information will help you to understand the actual costs of the lease you are considering.

Free copies of this checklist can be obtained through most state consumer protection agencies. Or you can order them for $1.50 per copy by sending a self-addressed, stamped envelope to:

CTF REALITY CHECKLIST
P.O. Box 7648
Atlanta, GA 30357

9

At the End of the Lease: "To Buy or Not to Buy"

When you've reached the end of the lease, should you purchase the vehicle? That depends. Unless you were tricked into leasing by a really slick salesman, you're probably more interested in driving a new car every two or three years (no matter how much more that costs). If that describes you—the "ideal lease customer"—then turn the car in and lease another new one.

On the other hand, if you normally prefer to buy and keep a vehicle for at least four or five years, but you were lured by one of those "zero down, $199 a month" bargain leases, you might be considering the purchase option at the end of your lease. Should you exercise the option?

To make an intelligent decision regarding the exercise of a purchase option, you need to research the actual market value of the vehicle and compare that to the residual amount. (The "purchase option" or "lease-end" amount is usually the same as the residual, but in some cases they may differ. Be sure to check your contract.) A substantial difference between residual and actual market values often exists—in spite of the fact that some salespeople have said there's a "guaranteed future value" for their vehicles. (That was just a sleazy sales trick.)

Warning: Inflated Residuals

If your initial lease was a good deal—for you, not the dealer—the vehicle will usually be worth less than the residual, sometimes much less. In that case, you would be foolish to purchase it for the residual amount. However, uninformed people make this mistake every day, to the good fortune of the automakers and leasing companies.

As mentioned in Chapter 3, a recent *Automotive News* story told how inflated residuals were causing Lincoln-Mercury (a division of Ford) to lose money on off-lease Lincolns. According to the article, late-model Lincolns were selling at auction for $1,000 to $5,000 below anticipated residual values, so the company allowed dealers to buy off-lease Lincolns for less than the residual amounts to keep them out of auctions.

However, the article said that dealers weren't interested in buying off-lease vehicles from Lincoln because they could buy the same cars at auction for as much as $1,500 below the company's discounted price. A company official confirmed that their dealers preferred to buy through auctions.

What's interesting about this story is that it reveals

how Ford (through its Lincoln-Mercury Division) had inflated residuals on those cars to the point that the company was losing as much as $5,000 per car at auction. Obviously, if you were to buy one of these at the residual amount, you would be paying a lot more than it's worth. How much more? Again, that depends.

Auction prices are wholesale values, which are always a lot lower than retail (the price a dealer may get from an uninformed buyer). And the selling prices found among private parties usually fall somewhere between wholesale and retail. Since the difference between retail and wholesale on a Lincoln can be as much as $4,000 to $5,000 you could be overpaying by as much as $3,000 to $4,000 if you purchase at the inflated residual amount.

Two more examples of Ford using inflated residuals are the 1994 Taurus and 1993 Tracer from the lawsuit mentioned in Chapter 3. The residuals were inflated by 17% on the Tracer and 9% on the Taurus. Even though a Taurus retails for almost twice as much as a Tracer, both cars had their residuals inflated by $1,600 to $1,700 (over average auction prices).

Inflating residuals is a common practice in the leasing business, not only at Ford, but at many other automakers (and lease companies) as well. Why? Because it helps to lower monthly payments, making leases more attractive. Unfortunately, many consumers are not aware of this practice and they make the mistake of purchasing at the residual amount.

Negotiate Your Purchase Price

Most people think that the residual/purchase option price is not negotiable, but it usually is. (The lenders just don't want you to know — they would rather sell you the car at full price than face their residual losses at auction.) To avoid paying more than a vehicle is really worth, be sure to do your homework on residual, wholesale, and retail values. If you're still serious about buying the vehicle (after finding out what it's really worth), negotiate the purchase price just as you would with any new or used car.

First, check out the residual numbers published in the *Automotive Lease Guide.* (See Chapter 8: "Resources," or try your local library or bank.) This is the easiest way to get accurate information on auction results. For example, if your three-year lease on a 1994 model started in November of 1993, you would look in the November 1996 book for the residual value of the 1997 model. The published residual in that book would represent the current, average (lease-end) auction price of your model—in average condition and within the mileage limits.

You can also check the retail and wholesale/trade-in numbers published in guide books by N.A.D.A., Pace, Edmunds, and others (at your local library, bookstore, or bank). However, keep in mind that their wholesale or trade-in numbers are usually higher than auction prices because they're for cars in "good/clean" condition, instead of "average." (And because auctions are the buyers of last resort.) The retail numbers are useful, too, because if you pay anywhere near retail, you're not getting a good deal.

About 30 days before the end of your lease, call the lender and tell them you would like to buy the car, but you know it's not worth the residual/purchase option amount. Make your first offer the same as the auction (wholesale) price, even if it's several thousand dollars below the residual. If they reject your offer, tell them to name the lowest price they would accept, then tell them you'll think it over and call them back if you're interested.

Wait two weeks, then call back to ask if they've reconsidered your original offer. If you're lucky, they might have a change of heart and take it—after all, if you don't buy the car, they'll get it back in two weeks. Then they have to store it, clean it up, take it to auction, and hope they get more than you offered to pay. (But they know they might not be that lucky.) So, if you've done your homework properly, hold out for a great price until the last few days of the lease. Chances are the lender will give in before you do.

Bargains: The Exception

In some (very rare) cases, your vehicle may be worth more at the end of the lease than the residual amount that was set by the lender, in which case you might actually end up with a bargain by purchasing for the residual amount. However, that end-of-lease "bargain" may not make up for the bad deal you probably got in the first place. (If the residual was set that low, your down payment and/or monthly payments were probably too high.)

Should you end up with a vehicle that's worth a lot more than the purchase option, but you really don't want to keep it, you may be tempted to buy it for the purpose of a quick and profitable resale. Before doing this, be sure to check with your state's motor vehicle department to see if both you and the new buyer will have to pay sales tax on the vehicle. If you do, most of the profits could end up in the state treasury instead of your pocket.

In any case, before you can resell the vehicle, you will usually have to exercise your option by purchasing it, paying any applicable sales tax, and taking possession. (If you're lucky, a quick resale might only require sales tax to be paid on one sale. Be sure to ask about this first.) To protect yourself, have your buyer lined up and ready to go—with a written agreement and a deposit to keep him from backing out—before exercising your option. Then proceed with the transaction.

Sorry to be a wet blanket, but your profits are probably considered taxable income. (Ask your accountant.) *I guess there's no such thing as "easy money," after all.*

10

"Single-Payment" or Prepaid Leases

An unadvertised gimmick offered by some dealers and/or manufacturers is the "single-payment," or prepaid lease. Instead of making payments every month, the customer makes one (very) large initial payment, with no other payments due for the remainder of the lease. Technically, the single payment is just a cap reduction that's large enough to reduce the monthly payments to zero.

This option seems to contradict the basic premise of leasing, which is supposed to be lower up-front costs to drive a car. In fact, if you have enough cash to prepay a lease (usually 40-50% of the cap cost), you will almost always be better off purchasing instead. Why? Since you're not paying off as much principal on a lease, you'll pay a lot more interest. (It's similar to making minimum payments on a credit card—the debt takes longer to pay off, and more interest is charged.)

For example, let's take a $20,000 car and compare a lease with a purchase, both at 8% for 36 months. Using zero down and a residual of 50%, the total finance charges on the lease would be $4,040 (including an acquisition fee of $450). On the loan, total finance charges would only be $2,565.

If we decided to prepay that lease, we would have to make a $12,127 cap reduction to eliminate the monthly payment. Since only $10,000 of that is depreciation, that leaves $2,127 for prepaid finance charges. (Yes, we still have to pay finance charges because they're based on the whole cap cost, not just the depreciation.) Counting the acquisition fee, total finance charges for the prepaid lease would be $2,577.

Notice that the total finance charges on the lease are still more than the loan interest—even after prepaying 50% of the car. If you had purchased instead, with 50% down, the total finance charges (over 36 months) would only be $1,282.

As you can see, a prepaid lease doesn't make as much sense as a prepaid purchase, so the major selling point would have to be convenience: no more monthly payments to mail, and no used car to sell (or trade) at the end. And, since a prepaid lease would require the customer to write one huge check, it would probably only appeal to someone with enough money to lease (or buy) a luxury vehicle.

So, if you're going to lease anyway, is prepayment a good idea? It depends on the interest rate you're paying, the size of the prepayment discount, and the amount of interest that could be earned on the money if it was invested instead.

Generally speaking, the higher the rate you're being charged on the vehicle, and the lower the rate you're earning on your investment, the more sense it makes to prepay. If both rates are the same, it may be a toss-up.

Evaluating a Single-Payment Lease

To evaluate a single-payment lease, you first need to figure out how much of a cap reduction is required to reduce the monthly payment to zero. Of course, the dealer will provide a figure, but you may want to calculate it yourself to determine if any discount is being offered. The easiest way to do that is with leasing software like Expert Lease Pro (see Chapter 8), but it can be done with a calculator and lots of scratch paper. (See "Calculating the Single-Payment Amount" at the end of this chaper.)

Once you have the necessary cap reduction, you can compare it to the prepayment amount to see if they're offering a discount. (Don't expect much.) The bigger the discount, the more attractive it would be to prepay.

Now you can calculate how much investment interest the money would earn if you didn't use it on the vehicle. There are two ways of looking at this: The first way is to figure that the invested prepayment amount will be gradually reduced to make the monthly payments. The second way is to figure that the invested amount will be left untouched for the whole term (for example, in a certificate of deposit or a mutual fund), and the monthly payments will be made from sources that have little-or-no return on investment (like a normal checking account).

Calculated the first way, the results will be similar to comparing the APRs of the lease and the investment: the lower the investment rate compared to the lease rate, the more money you would save by prepaying. However, if both rates are the same, the invested prepayment amount comes out slightly ahead because of the "time value of money," which will be explained in the next section. To calculate the return on a declining balance, you'll either need a computer program or a lot of spare time. (I used Expert Lease.)

Calculated the second way, with the investment left untouched for the whole term, the total return on the invested money can be higher than the prepayment savings, even if the investment rate is three or four percentage points lower than the lease rate. (That's because the invested balance is constant, while the lease balance is declining. Also, the time value of money benefits the invested amount.) If you can invest your money this way, you'll usually do better than someone who takes the prepayment option.

The Time Value of Money

The time value of money refers to this economic principle: *The value of a given sum of money depends on when the money is paid (or received).* In other words, a dollar today does not have the same value as a dollar twenty years later—it's worth more now. Why? Without taking inflation into account, money received today can be invested so that it will be worth more in the future.

When small amounts of money are involved over short periods of time, or interest/inflation rates are low, the time value concept does not usually have a significant effect on total costs or investment returns. It does, however, become very important when large sums of money are involved, interest rates/inflation are high, or longer periods of time apply. For example, the return on $1,000 after one year at 5% is only $50. After 10 years, the total return would be $629.

Because of the amount of money that's involved in a prepaid lease, it's important to understand and consider the time value concept. The following explanation and examples are provided to help you decide which option makes the most economic sense for your situation:

To calculate the time value of money, use the following formula ("F" is the future value, "P" is the present value, "i" is the annual rate of interest, and "n" is the length of time, in years):

$$F = P \times (1+i)^n$$

For example, let's take a hypothetical 36 month lease with monthly payments of $400 and no cap reduction. We are currently earning 4% interest on our savings, and are considering a single-payment lease on a new car. The total of payments would normally be $14,400 but the dealer said the prepaid amount would only be $13,200. Here's how to figure out whether that would be a good deal:

We would be taking the $13,200 out of an investment that is earning 4% so we need to figure out how much interest we would lose over the 36 months. Using the formula, the present value becomes $13,200 and the interest rate will be .04 (for 4%). Since the length of time is three years (from the 36 month lease), we replace "n" with 3. Here's how the formula looks now:

$$F = 13,200 \times (1+.04)^3$$

To solve this, (1+.04) becomes (1.04), which we multiply by itself three times:

$$(1+.04)^3 = 1.04 \times 1.04 \times 1.04 = \underline{1.124864}$$

Now we have:

$$F = 13,200 \times 1.124864 = \underline{14,848}$$

So the future value of the $13,200 (using an interest rate of only 4%) is $14,848 which is more than the total of monthly payments ($14,400). This means that the prepayment is not a good deal because it would cost us $448 in lost interest ($14,848 minus $14,400). A better deal would be a prepayment with a future value that was less than the total payments.

We can also change our formula to calculate a present value, which would tell us exactly how much the prepayment should be to avoid any lost income. Here's our new formula:

$$P = \frac{F}{(1+i)^n}$$

The prepayment amount (present value) that would grow to $14,400 (future value, after 3 years at 4%) is $12,802. Anything above that will cause lost income, and anything below it would be a good deal.

If we used an interest rate of 5% (which would be fairly easy to get with a bank certificate of deposit), the present value changes to $12,439. As you can see, the higher the interest rate you are earning on your money, the bigger the discount it will take to make prepaying attractive.

Calculating the Single-Payment Amount

Make sure you've read Chapter 4 ("How to Figure Lease Payments") so you understand the procedure. You can also use Worksheet #2 ("Lease Payment Calculation") from the Appendix.

Without software, you'll have to guess at the cap reduction amount until the monthly payment is reduced to zero, but here's a good starting point: Start a little higher than halfway between the total depreciation (net cap cost minus residual) and the total of all monthly lease payments.

For example, let's use a 36-month lease with a cap cost of $20,000 and a residual of $10,000. Using an APR of 8%, the monthly payment (with no cap reduction) is $377.51 so the total of payments is $13,590. The total depreciation is $10,000. Halfway between $13,590 and $10,000 is $11,795 and we want to start a little higher than halfway, so we'll round that up to an even $12,000. This will be our initial guess at the cap reduction.

If the cap reduction amount is greater than (or equal to) the total lease depreciation, two things happen when using our formula to figure monthly payments: the lease rate is significantly reduced and the monthly depreciation disappears. Here's how to use the formula on the prepayment in our example:

First, our $12,000 prepayment is greater than the total lease depreciation (which is only $10,000). By applying $10,000 of our prepayment to depreciation, we reduce that part of the monthly payment to zero. The remaining $2,000 will be applied to the monthly lease rate, so we'll divide the $2,000 by 36 (for the number of months in the lease) to get $55.55 per month in prepaid finance charges. We'll use that figure to reduce the lease rate in the next step.

When calculating the monthly lease rate, we have to reduce the cap cost to $10,000 (because we're prepaying all of the depreciation) before adding it to the residual and multiplying by .00333 (the money factor for 8%). So the new monthly lease rate is (10,000 + 10,000) times .00333 which equals $66.60. From that, we subtract

$55.55 (the prepaid finance charges from the previous step) and we get a lease payment of $11.05 per month.

Instead of zero, we still have a small monthly payment, so we need to increase the amount of our cap reduction. How much? Since we were only off by $11 a month, we should add $100 and run the numbers through the formula again.

Our initial guess was close—the exact cap reduction needed is $12,127. We could have arrived there eventually using our formula, raising (or lowering) the cap reduction until the monthly payment was zero, but it would take some time. (That's why I used Expert Lease—it's a lot faster. And it also tells me the future value of the money that's involved, using different investment rates.)

11

The Used-Car Lease

By late 1996, the used-car market was already showing signs of cooling down. The rapid growth of leasing resulted in a flood of late-model vehicles hitting the market, as most lease customers (over 85%) decided to turn in their cars instead of buying them. Adding to the problem was the availability of so many low-payment leases on new cars that used cars became less attractive.

After five straight years of increases, used-car prices appear to be leveling off, and the percentage of unsold vehicles at auctions has gone up. This could cause greater losses for automakers and lease companies as their vehicles bring less money at auction than they had anticipated.

What does all this mean to consumers? It means that automakers and leasing companies are going to have a tougher time getting decent prices for all those off-lease vehicles, so they had to figure out a way to prop up prices and move vehicles at the same time. "The used-car lease" was created to help move some of those unsold vehicles into the hands of paying customers, and automakers are creating "certified-vehicle" programs to help cure the price problem.

"The Used-Car Lease"

To unload some of those off-lease cars, automakers and leasing companies have come up with a brilliant idea: "the used-car lease." That's right, they're going to lease the same vehicle to someone else! After the first customer pays off 40-50% of the car, they turn around and lease it to customer #2 for 70-80% of original retail. Then he pays off another 50-60% and returns the car so they can sell it to someone else. Pretty good trick, isn't it? And it gives dealers a chance to make enormous profits on extended warranties, too!

In theory, used-car leasing should have an advantage over new-car leasing (or buying). Since lease payments are based (partly) on the price of a vehicle, the monthly payments should be lower on used cars because they cost less than new ones.

Turn to Table 1 ("Monthly Lease Payments") in the Appendix, and notice the effect price has on the monthly payment. For example, a new car that sells for $25,000 would have a monthly lease payment of $472 (36 month term, residual of 50% and APR of 8%). If you leased the same car—at the same terms—when it was 3 years old and selling for $14,000 (allowing a $1,500 profit for the dealer), the lease payment would only be $264.

That being said, we must now face the real world of car sales and leasing. The best deals on new-car leases are those with huge manufacturer subsidies that lower the monthly payments, and you'll probably never see one of those on a used car. In addition, there are three more things that can prevent those theoretical savings from being realized: the actual price of the car, the cost of maintenance and repairs, and the cost of an extended warranty to cover major expenses.

The "Cap Cost Mistake"

This truth from new-car leasing applies to used cars as well: *The knowledge and negotiating skill of the consumer will determine how good (or bad) the final deal turns out to be.* Since most people don't understand how leasing works, dealers usually get away with using higher cap costs than informed consumers would allow. To make matters worse, most consumers are also unaware of how much markup there is on used cars, so even when they do negotiate, they usually end up paying too much.

In our previous example, we said the payment should only be $264 on the used-car lease, but that was based on a cap cost of $14,000 (a markup of $1,500). It would be fairly easy for a dealer to use a cap cost of $18,000 (undisclosed, of course) because the monthly payment would only be $340. (See Table 1.) That's still $132 less than the payment on a new one—and the dealer would use that "logic" in his sales pitch.

Even though that deal may sound OK (the monthly payment *is* lower), it's horrible. The vehicle is only worth around $13,000 to $14,000 so the payment should be no more than $264. If you agreed to pay $340 per month on this lease, you would be (in effect) agreeing to a price of $18,000 on a $14,000 car.

115

To keep this from happening to you, do your home-work on wholesale and auction prices before signing any contracts (see Chapter 9), and be sure to figure out your own lease payment. Watch out for undisclosed interest rate hikes, too—they can have the same effect as a higher cap cost. (See Chapter 2 and Table 3.)

Maintenance & Repairs

One of the disadvantages of used-car leasing is the added expense of maintenance and repairs. Tune-ups, new tires, brakes, belts and hoses, radiator flushes, etc.—these can all add up to $1,000 (or more) for repairs that most cars will need between 30,000 and 60,000 miles. Spread out over the term of a lease, this $1,000 means an extra $42 per month for two years, or $28 per month for three years. And that's just for "expected" maintenance and re-pairs! Unexpected problems in the engine, transmission, and/or computer system could easily cost another $1,000 to $2,000.

That may not be a lot to spend on a car you own if it means that you can drive it for a few more years. But how are you going to feel spending money on a car you don't own? Especially if you have to give it back right af-ter paying for major repairs?

In case you're thinking that you can let some of those repairs go, a lease requires you to maintain the vehicle in good condition. If you don't, you can be charged for "ex-cess wear and tear" and/or "improper maintenance" at the end of the lease. You can't avoid maintenance and repair costs, so be sure to include those expenses when calculat-ing the total cost of a used-car lease.

And that brings us to another potential pitfall of used-car leasing: paying for extended warranties to cover ma-jor repair bills.

Extended Warranties

If you decide to lease a used car, what should you do about those unexpected repairs? Hang a rabbit's foot on your rearview mirror and hope you don't have any? Or should you buy an extended warranty to make sure any major repairs are covered? Well, dealers are hoping that most people will buy the warranties because it gives them another chance to make enormous profits.

Extended warranties for used cars usually contain a large markup (profit) for the dealer. Low-priced ones are often sold for $1,000 to $1,500 when their cost is only $300 or $400. And some higher-priced ones are sold for as much as $2,800 when the dealer's cost is only $1,000 to $1,400. (If you decide to get one, be sure to negotiate; try to pay no more than 50% of the dealer's asking price.)

Keep in mind that extended warranties will not cover the normal "wear-and-tear" items we just discussed (tires, brakes, tune-ups, etc.), so you'll still have to pay for those even if you have a warranty. Adding a $1,500 warranty to normal maintenance costs of $1,000 causes the total cost of driving to increase by $105 per month on a two-year lease, or $70 per month on a three-year lease, so be sure to include those expenses in your evaluation.

Another problem with buying an extended warranty on a used car is that it may turn out to be worthless. The warranty company might refuse to pay for needed repairs by claiming that the problem was caused by something else that the warranty doesn't cover. For example, if your warranty says, "Does not cover gaskets and seals," a seal or gasket could blow out, causing a loss of oil followed by severe damage to the engine or transmission. That one clause could give the company an excuse to refuse payment, leaving you with a huge repair bill.

To avoid that, look for a warranty that covers whole

assemblies (engines, transmissions, etc.) instead of only specific internal parts. Policies that provide "bumper-to-bumper" coverage (excluding normal maintenance items) are your best bet.

Watch out for "50-50" policies that require you to pay half of the repair bill (usually at the dealer's shop, or one they've selected). These are often worthless because they can inflate the actual charges so that the "half" you pay ends up covering the whole repair.

Worse yet, the company could go out of business before your warranty expires, leaving you with nothing but a worthless piece of paper. (That's happened at several warranty companies already.) Make sure that a warranty is backed by a reputable company that's been in business for at least ten years.

To protect yourself on a used-car lease, tell the dealer that you expect him to provide an extended warranty for free, or you don't want the car. (If that doesn't work, you might offer to pay $200 to $300 for it, but make sure it's a legitimate warranty.) The warranty should have a low deductible and it should provide coverage for the term of the lease.

"Certified Vehicle" Programs With (Usually) Free Warranties

Several automakers have already announced their plans to operate "certified vehicle" programs for their off-lease cars. After undergoing a thorough inspection (followed by any necessary reconditioning), select low-mileage vehicles will be covered by an extended factory warranty ranging from 1 year/12,000 miles (on Fords) to as much as 6 years/100,000 miles (on Toyotas).

Most warranties will be provided to customers free of charge, and some automakers may offer a brief money-back guarantee that would allow buyers to return their vehicles for a full refund if they're not satisfied. (This might help their dealers to compete with used-car "super-stores" like CarMax and AutoNation.)

Final Notes

Since the real owners of leased vehicles are the leasing companies, they don't want to see their cars come back in need of repairs. And they would rather not have to sue their customers to recover repair costs—but they will if they have to. To encourage people to get extended warranties on used cars, many lenders will offer better deals on cars that have this coverage (and worse deals on cars that don't).

Don't automatically assume that a lease is a good deal because the warranty is included: they might be inflating the price of the car to cover it. Make sure you research the wholesale and retail values of a vehicle, and perform your own lease calculations, before signing any contracts.

When you add up all the costs of leasing a used car (including maintenance and repairs), you might find that you could get a better deal on a new car with a factory-subsidized lease. If you're still determined to lease a used car, a "certified vehicle" with a free warranty could turn out to be your best bet, especially if the warranty lasts as long as the lease.

12

The Future of Leasing?

New-car leasing has experienced record growth over the last five years, and a number of people have predicted that it will continue to increase until it reaches 50% of all new vehicle transactions. (As recently as 1990, only 13% of all new cars and light trucks were leased. That figure grew to over 32% by 1996.) However, some industry analysts don't think that will happen; they expect leasing to peak around 38-40%.

If manufacturers, dealers, and consumers all (supposedly) love leasing, why wouldn't it continue to grow at its present rate? Because the "success story" of leasing in the 1990's is due to a number of conditions that may not exist in the future: rising used-car prices, limited disclosure (and poor public understanding) of important leasing terms, generous manufacturer incentives/subsidies, few investigations or lawsuits over leasing abuses, and poor consumer awareness concerning fraud in the sales/leasing business.

Falling Used Car Prices

A major factor that allowed manufacturers (and lease companies) to offer better lease deals was a four-year period of increasing used-car prices. Prior to 1991, year-to-year prices for used cars were typically flat, or they only dropped a few percent. But prices started increasing in 1991 and averaged about 8% higher every year for the next three years. Since vehicles were selling for higher prices at auction, this prompted leasing companies to raise their residuals which lowered the monthly lease payments.

In my last book, *What Car Dealers Don't Want You to Know*, I said that used-car price increases could not continue at that rate or used cars would end up costing more than new ones. (New-car prices had only been increasing 2-3% every year.) I also said that a flood of off-lease used cars that was expected to hit the market in 1997 (about 3 million vehicles) could depress used-car prices and cause losses for lenders who had been betting on higher residual values.

Well, it looks like that scenario may be coming true. In 1995, price increases for used cars had slowed to 4% and it looks like 1996 will end with no increase at all (or possibly a 1% drop). What this means for the leasing industry is that it will be even more expensive for lenders to offer low-priced deals. Lower used-car prices will force lenders to reduce the residuals on most of their leases, causing the payments to go up, or the manufacturers will have to spend more money on subsidies to make their leases attractive.

To help prop up used-car prices, manufacturers are expected to come out with more national programs that offer warranties on their best used vehicles. Ford Motor Co. recently announced a test program on certified used cars and trucks, but they were not the first one—Toyota's certified used vehicle program is already offered nationwide. Besides helping to maintain good used car prices, these programs also help dealers compete with the new, used-car "superstores" (like CarMax and AutoNation).

Reduced Manufacturer Subsidies

As manufacturers experience greater losses at auctions (because of their inflated residuals), they may decide against offering generous lease subsidies in the future. Even if residual losses are considered manageable, the companies still end up with drastically-reduced profits from widespread use of subsidies. And heavy use of subsidized leasing can erode the prices of new and used cars.

For example, an October 28, 1996 story in *Automotive News* detailed General Motors' plans to cut back on its leasing subsidies. GM said it had ended incentive payments to repeat lease customers, cut back on residual and lease rate subsidies, and stopped payments to dealers for staff training in leasing. Cadillac is now offering its lease customers $2,000 if they buy their next one instead of leasing it.

GM's recent decision will no doubt make many of their leases less attractive. Whether shoppers end up buying a GM car instead of leasing it, or they decide to lease from a competitor who offers lower payments, the reduced subsidies should cause a drop in GM's leasing business. If other automakers also decide to cut back, shoppers might have to look a little harder to find great lease deals in the future. Of course, even if automakers do cut back on subsidized "bargain" leases, they will probably revert to them the next time new-car sales drop off.

Investigations & Lawsuits

There has a been a lot of fraud in the new-car leasing business, but only two major investigations have been concluded and publicized so far (the Florida investigation targeting Toyota dealers and the false advertising charges against five automakers over their "no money down" leases). Other investigations and class-action lawsuits are under way.

As more leasing investigations and lawsuits are settled, lease companies (and dealers) will be forced to change the way they do business. More disclosure will be required, some types of deceptive advertising will no longer be used, and fraudulent sales tactics should be less common.

Disclosure & Consumer Awareness

One reason for the success of leasing is that most people who lease don't understand how it works. That's why so many people lease (at MSRP or higher) without trying to negotiate a better deal, while others make large down payments without receiving the proper reduction in their monthly payments. Many have been victimized by some type of leasing fraud, but few have any idea they were cheated, or by how much.

In the future, more disclosure combined with greater public awareness could put the brakes on leasing's rapid growth.

Summary

After reading this book, you now know how to tell the honest salesmen from the "morally-challenged." When you find an honest dealer, tell everyone you know—and do the same when you find a dishonest one.

You also know how to make dealers compete for your business, which is the only way to get the best deal. Remember this: *The knowledge and negotiating skill of the consumer will determine how good (or bad) the final deal turns out to be.*

If you lease, make sure it's a "closed-end" one, for no longer than 3 years. And be on the lookout for hidden price increases: there's no federal requirement to disclose cap cost until October of 1997. After that date, dealers will still be able to hide the interest rates they're charging on leases, so watch out for secret APR increases.

Note to Victims of Leasing Fraud

If you think that you were cheated on a lease, here's what you should do: Use the worksheets in the Appendix to figure out what your lease payment should be. If you were overcharged by more than 5% of MSRP from a secret price boost, stolen down payment or trade-in, etc., make two copies of the worksheets, your lease contract, window sticker (or MSRP info), and a letter explaining what happened. Make sure your name, address, and phone number are in the letter. Mail one copy to your state's attorney general, then mail the other copy to the author at the following address: TechNews Publishing, 7840 Madison Ave., Ste. 185, Fair Oaks, CA 95628.

Open Letter
to
Ford Motor Co.
&
All Ford/Lincoln-Mercury Dealers

To the honest dealers:

I know this book will create a hardship for those of you who did not "participate" in the leasing schemes because you are honest people. However, if enough of you had tried, you could have stopped the deceptive training eight years ago, before thousands of people were cheated.

Isn't it time to stand up and do the right thing? Tell the company—and the "other" dealers—to come clean. If they don't, your reputations and businesses may be seriously damaged, and you will have no one to blame but yourselves.

To Ford Motor Co. & "participating" dealers:

Your customers worked hard for their money; they trusted you and did not deserve to be cheated like that. *Give the money back!*

126

Appendix

Worksheet #1 — Lease Information

Vehicle year, make, model _____

Retail price (MSRP) _____

Vehicle Price:

A. Negotiated vehicle price _____

B. Add-ons: (warranty, insurance, etc.)

_____

C. Gross cap cost (A+B)   _____

Credits:

D. Cash down payment   _____

E. Net trade-in allowance _____

F. Rebates   _____

G. Total cap cost reduction (D+E+F)   _____

Lease Terms:

Net cap cost (C minus G)   _____

Term _____ Money factor _____ Interest rate _____

Monthly payment _____ Residual value _____

H. Total of monthly payments   _____

Amounts due at lease signing:

Cash down payment (optional)   _____

Net trade-in allowance (optional)   _____

Refundable security deposit   _____

1) Acquisition fee   _____

2) Title/registration fees   _____

3) Sales tax on cap reduction (G)   _____

First month's payment   _____

Total due at lease signing   _____

Total cost of lease (G+H+1+2+3)   _____

Worksheet #2 — Lease Payment Calculation

Part 1: Monthly Depreciation
[Term is the length of the lease in months.]
Monthly Depreciation =
$\qquad$ (Net Cap Cost — Residual) ÷ Term

Net Cap Cost	_____
Minus Residual	_____
Total	_____
÷ Term	_____
Monthly Depreciation	_____

Part 2: Lease Rate (Monthly Finance Charge)
Money Factor = APR [.xxx] ÷ 24
Lease Rate = (Net Cap Cost + Residual) X Money Factor

Net Cap Cost	_____
Plus Residual	_____
Total	_____
Times Money Factor	_____
Monthly Lease Rate	_____

Part 3: Total Monthly Payment
Monthly Payment = Monthly Depreciation + Lease Rate
(Plus applicable sales tax on the total monthly payment)

Monthly Depreciation	_____
Plus Monthly Lease Rate	_____
Monthly Payment	_____
(Plus Sales Tax)	_____
(Monthly Payment w/Tax)	_____

Worksheet #3 — Purchase Information

Vehicle year, make, model _____

Retail price (MSRP) _____

Vehicle Price:

A. Negotiated vehicle price _____

B. Add-ons: (warranty, insurance, etc.)

_____

C. <u>Total purchase price</u> (A+B)   _____

Credits:

D. Cash down payment   _____

E. Net trade-in allowance _____

F. Rebates   _____

G. <u>Total credits</u> (D+E+F)   _____

Financing:

<u>Loan amount</u> (C minus G)   _____

Term _____ Interest rate _____

Monthly payment _____

H. <u>Total of monthly payments</u>   _____

Amounts due at loan signing:

Cash down payment (optional)   _____

Net trade-in allowance (optional)   _____

1) Title/registration fees   _____

2) Sales tax   _____

<u>Total due at loan signing</u>   _____

Total cost of purchase (G+H+1+2)   _____

<u>Minus equity at end of term</u>   _____

Net cost of purchase   _____

Payment Tables

The following tables of lease and loan payments are provided for educational purposes; they are not meant to cover all possible lease or loan situations.

Your actual payments may vary, depending on the negotiated price, down payment, trade-in, rebate, interest rate, residual, and length of lease (or loan). Since the possible combinations of factors are virtually unlimited, it would not be practical to attempt listing them in print.

To calculate the monthly payments for combinations not listed here, use the preceding worksheets and the procedure outlined in Chapter 4, "How to Figure Lease Payments." Or you can use the computer program I used: "Expert Lease Pro" by CHART Software. (See Chapter 8, "The Homework Section," for more information on this program.)

Table 1

LEASE

Monthly Lease Payments
$10,000 to $25,000 Cap Cost (Price)
8% APR, 0 Down

Cap Cost	24 mos.	36 mos.	48 mos.
10,000	219	189	172
11,000	241	208	189
12,000	263	227	206
13,000	285	245	224
14,000	307	264	241
15,000	329	283	258
16,000	351	302	275
17,000	373	321	292
18,000	395	340	310
19,000	417	359	327
20,000	439	378	344
21,000	461	396	361
22,000	483	415	378
23,000	505	434	396
24,000	527	453	413
25,000	549	472	430

(Amounts rounded to nearest dollar.)
Residuals: 60% (24 mos.), 50% (36 mos.), 40% (48 mos.)

Table 2

PURCHASE

Monthly Loan Payments
$10,000 to $25,000 Loan Amounts
8% APR

Loan Amount	36 mos.	48 mos.	60 mos.
10,000	313	244	203
11,000	345	269	223
12,000	376	293	243
13,000	407	317	264
14,000	439	342	284
15,000	470	366	304
16,000	501	391	324
17,000	533	415	345
18,000	564	439	365
19,000	595	464	385
20,000	627	488	406
21,000	658	513	426
22,000	689	537	446
23,000	721	562	466
24,000	752	586	487
25,000	783	610	507

(Amounts rounded to nearest dollar.)

Table 3

LEASE

Monthly Lease Payments
Based on APR Changes
$20,000 Cap Cost (Price)
7% to 12% APR, 0 Down

APR	24 mos.	36 mos.	48 mos.
7%	426	365	332
8%	439	378	344
9%	452	390	356
10%	465	403	368
11%	478	415	380
12%	492	428	392

(Amounts rounded to nearest dollar.)
Residuals: 60% (24 mos.), 50% (36 mos.), 40% (48 mos.)

Table 4

PURCHASE

Monthly Loan Payments
Based on APR Changes
$20,000 Loan Amount
7% to 12% APR

APR	36 mos.	48 mos.	60 mos.
7%	618	479	396
8%	627	488	406
9%	636	498	415
10%	645	507	425
11%	655	517	435
12%	664	527	445

(Amounts rounded to nearest dollar.)

Table 5

LEASE

Monthly Lease Payments
vs. Price Discounts/Down Payments
from MSRP of $20,000
8% APR, 0 Down

Cap Cost	24 mos.	36 mos.	48 mos.
18,000	349	315	296
18,500	371	331	308
19,000	394	346	320
19,500	416	362	332
20,000	439	378	344
20,500	461	393	356
21,000	484	409	368
21,500	506	424	380
22,000	529	440	392

(Amounts rounded to nearest dollar.)
A $1,000 price discount causes the same reduction in the monthly payment as a $1,000 down payment.
Residuals: 60% (24 mos.), 50% (36 mos.), 40% (48 mos.)

Table 6

LEASE

Monthly Lease Payments
vs. Price Discounts/Down Payments
from MSRP of $15,000
8% APR, 0 Down

Cap Cost	24 mos.	36 mos.	48 mos.
13,500	262	236	222
14,000	284	252	234
14,500	307	268	246
15,000	329	283	258
15,500	352	299	270
16,000	374	314	282
16,500	397	330	294

(Amounts rounded to nearest dollar.)
A $1,000 price discount causes the same reduction in the
monthly payment as a $1,000 down payment.
Residuals: 60% (24 mos.), 50% (36 mos.), 40% (48 mos.)

Table 7

LEASE

Monthly Lease Payments
vs. Price Discounts/Down Payments
from MSRP of $10,000
8% APR, 0 Down

Cap Cost	24 mos.	36 mos.	48 mos.
9,100	179	161	150
9,400	192	170	157
9,700	206	179	165
10,000	219	189	172
10,300	233	198	179
10,600	246	207	187
10,900	260	217	194

(Amounts rounded to nearest dollar.)
A $600 price discount causes the same reduction in the
monthly payment as a $600 down payment.
Residuals: 60% (24 mos.), 50% (36 mos.), 40% (48 mos.)

Table 8

LEASE

Monthly Lease Payments
Based on Residual Changes
$20,000 Cap Cost (Price)
8% APR, 0 Down

Residual	24 mos.	36 mos.	48 mos.
66%	393		
64%	408		
62%	424		
60%	439		
58%	454		
56%	470	348	
54%	485	358	
52%		368	
50%		378	
48%		387	
46%		397	323
44%		407	330
42%			337
40%			344
38%			351
36%			358
34%			365

(Amounts rounded to nearest dollar.)

Table 9

PURCHASE

Monthly Loan Payments
$10,000 to $25,000 Loan Amounts
7% to 12% APR
36 months

Loan Amount	7%	8%	9%	10%	11%	12%
10,000	309	313	318	323	327	332
11,000	340	345	350	355	360	365
12,000	371	376	382	387	393	399
13,000	401	407	413	419	426	432
14,000	432	439	445	452	458	465
15,000	463	470	477	484	491	498
16,000	494	501	509	516	524	531
17,000	525	533	541	549	557	565
18,000	556	564	572	581	589	598
19,000	587	595	604	613	622	631
20,000	618	627	636	645	655	664
21,000	648	658	668	678	688	698
22,000	679	689	700	710	720	731
23,000	710	721	731	742	753	764
24,000	741	752	763	774	786	797
25,000	772	783	795	807	818	830

(Amounts rounded to nearest dollar.)

Table 10

PURCHASE

Monthly Loan Payments
$10,000 to $25,000 Loan Amounts
7% to 12% APR
48 months

Loan Amount	7%	8%	9%	10%	11%	12%
10,000	239	244	249	254	258	263
11,000	263	269	274	279	284	290
12,000	287	293	299	304	310	316
13,000	311	317	324	330	336	342
14,000	335	342	348	355	362	369
15,000	359	366	373	380	388	395
16,000	383	391	398	406	414	421
17,000	407	415	423	431	439	448
18,000	431	439	448	457	465	474
19,000	455	464	473	482	491	500
20,000	479	488	498	507	517	527
21,000	503	513	523	533	543	553
22,000	527	537	547	558	569	579
23,000	551	562	572	583	594	606
24,000	575	586	597	609	620	632
25,000	599	610	622	634	646	658

(Amounts rounded to nearest dollar.)

Table 11

PURCHASE

Monthly Loan Payments
$10,000 to $25,000 Loan Amounts
7% to 12% APR
60 months

Loan Amount	7%	8%	9%	10%	11%	12%
10,000	198	203	208	212	217	222
11,000	218	223	228	234	239	245
12,000	238	243	249	255	261	267
13,000	257	264	270	276	283	289
14,000	277	284	291	297	304	311
15,000	297	304	311	319	326	334
16,000	317	324	332	340	348	356
17,000	337	345	353	361	370	378
18,000	356	365	374	382	391	400
19,000	376	385	394	404	413	423
20,000	396	406	415	425	435	445
21,000	416	426	436	446	457	467
22,000	436	446	457	467	478	489
23,000	455	466	477	489	500	512
24,000	475	487	498	510	522	534
25,000	495	507	519	531	544	556

(Amounts rounded to nearest dollar.)

Another consumer book by

Mark Eskeldson

What Auto Mechanics Don't Want You to Know

LEARN ALL ABOUT:

Secret Warranties:
How to Get Free Repairs

Undercover Investigations:
Well-Known Repair Shops That Have Been Busted

Avoiding Repair Scams;
Getting Your Money Back

Finding Mechanics You Can Trust

Vehicle Maintenance Secrets

"...a better-informed consumer is less likely to be taken advantage of. And that's why Eskeldson wrote his book...Even if you don't have the time to spend reading...keep the book as a reference."
—*CAR AND DRIVER*

Technews Publishing, $11.95
ISBN 0-9640560-3-8

Both books available in bookstores
or call (800) 528-8634
All orders shipped within 3 days
Money-back Guarantee